Introducing New Approaches:
Improved Public Service Delivery

Published by: Commonwealth Secretariat
Marlborough House
Pall Mall
London SW1Y 5HX

Copyright   © Commonwealth Secretariat 1998

All Rights Reserved. No part of this publication may be reproduced, stored in a retrieval system, or transmitted in any form or by any means, electronic or mechanical, including photocopying, recording or otherwise, without prior permission of the publisher.

May be purchased from:
Commonwealth Association for Public Administration
(CAPAM)
150 Eglinton Avenue East, Suite 306
Toronto
Ontario
CANADA M4P 1E8

Telephone: 1 (416) 488 1504
Facsimile: 1 (416) 481 6510

or from the Commonwealth Secretariat's distributors:
Vale Packaging Ltd
420 Vale Road
Tonbridge
Kent TN9 1TD
Britain

Telephone: +44 (0) 1732 359387
Facsimile: +44 (0) 1732 770620

ISBN: 0 85092 564 9

Price: £9.00/US$14.00

Printed by the University of Toronto Press Inc.

Introducing New Approaches: Improved Public Service Delivery

Managing the Public Service
Strategies for Improvement Series: No. 5

Commonwealth Secretariat
1998

Online Research Library
Ministry of Education & Training
13th Floor, Mowat Block, Queen's Park
Toronto, Ontario M7A 1L2

FOREWORD

A strong and achieving public service is a necessary condition for a competitively successful nation. The Management and Training Services Division of the Commonwealth Secretariat assists member governments to improve the performance of the public service through action-oriented advisory services, policy analysis and training. This assistance is supported by funds from the Commonwealth Fund for Technical Co-operation (CFTC).

Commonwealth co-operation in public administration is facilitated immeasurably by the strong similarities that exist between all Commonwealth countries in relation to the institutional landscape and the underlying principles and values of a neutral public service. In mapping current and emerging best practices in public service management, the Management and Training Services Division has been able to draw on the most determined, experienced and successful practitioners, managers and policy-makers across the Commonwealth. Their experiences are pointing the way to practical strategies for improvement.

This new publication series, *Managing the Public Service: Strategies for Improvement*, provides the reader with access to the experiences and the successes of elected and appointed officials from across the Commonwealth.

The series complements other Management and Training Services Division publications, and very particularly the *Public Service Country Profile* series which provides a country-by-country analysis of current good practices and new developments in public service management. Our aim is to provide practical guidance and to encourage critical evaluation. The *Public Service Country Profile* series sets out the **where** and the **what** in public service management. With this new *Strategies for Improvement* series, I believe that we are providing the **how**.

Mohan Kaul
Director
Management and Training Services Division
Commonwealth Secretariat

ACKNOWLEDGEMENTS

This publication was made possible through the contributions of Jane Cole, consultant and John Shields, research associate. The Commonwealth Secretariat is grateful for their invaluable assistance. The Secretariat would like to express its gratitude to various Commonwealth governments for sharing information on recent developments in public service reform.

The Commonwealth Secretariat would like to thank Roy Chalmers for his assistance in the production of this series.

CONTENTS

The Context for Change	1
Managing Public Service Delivery	6
Improving Quality Management	13
Changing Organisational Culture	24
Mechanisms for Improving Service Delivery	28
The Role of Information Technology in Improving Service Delivery	49
Citizen Orientation	57
Improving Government Regulation	64
Conclusions	70
Bibliography	71

THE CONTEXT FOR CHANGE

Since the mid-1970s, governments have been increasingly concerned with adapting and developing the structures and values for the public service in order to achieve greater efficiency, and more responsive and flexible services. The origins of this movement lay in a combination of economic crisis and geo-political changes which led to reduced financial resources for governments. More recently though, it has also been pulled by a sense of new possibilities: the development of a new set of managerial strategies which promise better results from fewer resources. The successes of the first two decades of public service re-organisation have shown that, even in the absence of the pressures which first inspired them, these new approaches pay off by both reducing costs and improving service delivery. Today, public service reform is not so much an issue of political ideology as one of good governance and managerial expediency.

PRESSURES FOR CHANGE

The dismantling of large, centralised bureaucracies and the end of the 'command and control' system of public service management was based on principles borrowed from similar restructuring programmes in the private sector. The perceived need to downsize, privatise and rationalise public functions came from a number of pressures which include, but are not limited to, the following:

- globalisation and intensified international competition;

- increasing deficit and accumulated debt burdens; and

- changing public perceptions regarding the role and performance of public institutions and the services they deliver.

Globalisation

The growing interdependence among nations is well documented. Economic, social, environmental, labour and human rights issues have to be dealt with increasingly at an international level. International agreements bind national governments in various ways. Globalisation has thereby reduced the ability of individual governments to act alone. National interests have to be advanced through negotiation with other states, both bilaterally and through a complex network of transnational institutions.

Globalisation has meant that governments must constantly attempt to reconcile global imperatives with local needs, preserving the integrity, variety and uniqueness of national institutions in the face of the global forces of harmonisation. They have a key role to play in safeguarding the public good in the rush towards globalisation.

Intensified international competition is a key economic consequence of globalisation. This competition is not confined to the private sector as governments become more involved, highlighting the mutual dependence of the public and private sectors. Thus, government policy and service delivery have to take account of possible impacts of international competitiveness to an increasing degree. This can sometimes create tensions with environmental and social policy objectives, further adding to the complexities of governance and placing new demands on the policy co-ordination process.

National debt and economic pressures

During the previous two decades, the main impetus for changes in the role and responsibilities of government has come from economic pressures. The balance of payments deficits faced by many Commonwealth countries has eroded exchange rates and government purchasing power. Terms of trade have meant that developing countries could not cover their needs for imports of manufactured products. As many of the imports were needed by government itself, this was a crisis of national capacity as much as a restriction on consumers.

Increasing recourse to borrowing as a source of revenue for government led to levels of external and internal debt which were greater than total GDP. Noting this alarming trend somewhat belatedly, the lending institutions withdrew credit facilities during the 1980s. Subsequently, multilateral and bilateral agencies became more unwilling to provide funds for general budget purposes, thus sources of borrowing dried up dramatically. The resultant 'Third World debt crisis' of the early 1980s ensured that private sector bankers have been reluctant to provide further sovereign loans.

Debt reduces the government's fiscal capacity to sustain existing public service programmes and develop new ones. As a result, governments face difficult choices in allocating resources among different and often competing objectives. More than any other single factor, it has forced governments to identify and focus on their core responsibilities and to find ways of delivering services that consume less public money.

Changing public perceptions

The need for reductions in expenditure coupled with the persistently poor performance of public services was eroding confidence in the abilities of the government and the state-owned enterprises to provide the necessary goods and services for citizens. Government services have acquired a reputation world-wide, with a few notable exceptions, for poor products and attitudes.

At the same time, the public is demanding more transparency, accountability and integrity from government and calling for greater inclusion in political and bureaucratic decision-making. There is a perception that government should be run like a business with a focus on efficiency. While this may indicate a lack of public appreciation of the role of government and the importance of fairness, consistency and adherence to democratic principles, it may also reflect a failure on the part of government to demonstrate clearly how it adds to social and economic value and what results it has achieved. This has left the public service vulnerable to criticism and has added to its negative image.

Part of the difficulty is that public demands on government appear inconsistent. Demands for cost reductions cannot easily be reconciled with inclusiveness in decision-making and adherence to public values, such as fairness, consistency and the prudent use of public money. Further, because of their nature and complexity, many of the issues faced by government cannot be addressed in the manner of a private sector business.

INCENTIVES FOR CHANGE

Although rethinking the strategies of public service delivery was initially a response to the pressures described above, in recent years restructuring has been seen as an essential component of sound governance. Some of the incentives for reform include:

- rapid developments in information technology that have created many opportunities related to service delivery;

- the proven success of new and more effective management techniques borrowed from the private sector;

- the maximising of both financial and human resources; and

- an improved public perception of the services provided, and government itself.

Information Technology

The continuing pace of development in information technology and communication systems and applications has provided significant opportunities regarding the nature of work, both inside and outside the public service.

Information technology (combined with higher levels of education) has helped create a better-informed public in many countries which is pressing for greater direct involvement in the affairs of the state. Such involvement is greatly facilitated by new means of electronic access to government information, via the Internet for example. Ultimately, public service delivery can only improve as a result of this more direct interaction with its clients.

In addition to supporting policy development, information technology can enhance government efficiency and productivity, helping to integrate and speed up public service operations in any sector from the postal service to tax collection. The uninhibited exchange information across the country allows for a more effective devolvement of power and decentralisation of administration.

The freer flow of information also facilitates open government, supporting public values, such as transparency, probity, accountability, fairness and consistency.

Managerialism

The first two decades of experimentation with the downsizing, commercialisation, privatisation and the general re-ordering of the public service to behave more like a private enterprise has shown that, although initially inspired by financial constraints, these practices, when properly monitored, are not only cheaper but more effective.

The clear benefits of public service restructuring have also meant that the introduction of management principles from the private sector has ceased to be part of the ideological debate on the role of government in society. The close association between managerialism and 'new right' politics of the 1980s is now dissolving. Managerialism can now be seen as a way of improving public services, regardless of where governments are located on the political spectrum.

Finding alternative methods of delivering public service is no longer, then, a question of political philosophy. Now that the mould of unitary bureaucracy has been broken, it is possible to see the adoption by governments of strategies such as privatisation or the contracting out of services to private companies or non-governmental organisations (NGOs) in a different light. Such measures are now part of choosing the most efficient mechanisms for managing public service. Far from abdicating responsibility, a government which undertakes such measures is presiding over the prudent delegation of public service to those who can handle it more efficiently; and thus, ultimately, is better serving the public good.

Making the most of resources

Public service reform, as a result of having financial pressures as its starting point, has moved on to come to be about maximising the potential of the limited resources available.

Aside from such mechanisms as user-charging or privatisation which transfer the burden of service costs away from government, a variety of alternative strategies have been found for improving efficiency within those services still directly financed from the state coffers. Competitive tendering and market-testing ensure that public services use their budgets to the greatest effect, better guaranteeing value for money than the old bureaucratic systems.

Restructuring also concerns more effective management of human resources. Thus a move towards results-focused and values-based management tailored to the culture and circumstance of each country helps to increase motivation and efficiency amongst public servants. The effect of such new approaches on the delivery of services is especially valuable when dealing with personnel in direct contact with the public.

Improving public interface

This is one of the most formidable aspects of public service reform, since client response to changes in service delivery are somewhat paradoxical. As services become more efficient and citizens are invited to become active customers rather than passive recipients of government services, they tend to become more critical. Public services that perform poorly encourage public indifference and thus continued poor performance is tolerated. A reforming public sector finds itself under increasing pressure as it gets more efficient.

To operate effectively, though, governments need this pressure. Pressure creates an incentive for better performance, and thus it is in the interests of governments to put in place the mechanisms through which this pressure might be applied, not just at election time but consistently. Governments which can be perceived as working for their people will be more successful, even if public criticism increases, than those whose inertia generates public indifference.

MANAGING PUBLIC SERVICE DELIVERY

Current economic realities have led many governments to review the programmes they deliver and the way they deliver them. As a result, many governments are examining whether current programmes should continue to be delivered, and whether there are alternative methods of service delivery that are more responsive to the clients' needs, as well as being more cost-efficient and effective. The question for today's political leaders and public servants is not when or if to innovate, but how.

RECENT TRENDS

There are many different methods of service delivery, encompassing a wide range of activities, arrangements and financing options. These include corporatisation, contracting out, devolution and privatisation. The use of different forms of service delivery are part of a new public management paradigm aimed at fostering a performance-oriented culture in a less centralised public sector. The new public management provides innovative solutions to meeting the demands of the public who are increasingly aware of service delivery options and value for money.

Alternative methods of service delivery help contribute to public sector renewal through partnerships that share powers; by creating better accountability arrangements; by making better use of resources; by re-investing in quality services that are user-driven; through development of entrepreneurial action and through increased inter-jurisdictional co-operation. Thus, these options offer governments better insights into the relationship between the state and the public and provide opportunities to re-define these relations.

Currently, politicians and public servants across the Commonwealth are asking if there is a need for a range of possible service delivery options outside the traditional public service structures.

Historically, governments have focused their efforts on ensuring that public programmes and service delivery were consistent with prevailing public values, democratic principles and national policy objectives, with less attention being paid to efficiency considerations or the service requirements of clients. In most cases, programme delivery has focused on controlling input costs and responding to fixed, and at times, inflexible policy objectives, in addition to a range of supplementary objectives, such as removing regional disparities and promoting equal employment opportunities. Often the result was a set of common procedures and policies that failed to recognise or accommodate the specific needs of each programme and the clients it served.

In more recent decades, however, consumer groups have been set up which exert pressure on governments for improved public services. Now, in discussions at the decision-making level, it is apparent that more balance is needed between policy/political concerns and service delivery requirements of programme recipients, including the appropriateness of user fees and of new service delivery models, especially partnerships. Programme managers are shifting their focus away from inputs to programme outputs and outcomes.

The current emphasis on efficiency, downsizing and the potential of new technology has created a number of opportunities for public sector reform and renewal. Governments now find there is the political will and public support to implement significant, and in some cases, radical policy and programme changes. A recent study noted that, broadly speaking, governments have three different options regarding their future roles and responsibilities for programme activities:

- Relinquishing public policy obligations, devolution of responsibilities to others, or privatisation.

- Doing more with less – the continued maintenance of the public service by contracting out, by using structures within the bureaucracy, or by continuing to demand more output from the current work-force.

- Finding new ways of delivering public services by sharing governance functions with individuals, community groups, voluntary organisations and NGOs.

MECHANISMS FOR IMPROVING SERVICE DELIVERY

Governments have been experimenting with a wide range of institutional mechanisms to improve service delivery. Greater use of markets is creating competitive pressures and more alternatives to public provision for users seeking better quality or lower cost. Among these options is the practice of contracting out service delivery to private firms or NGOs. Some governments are setting up operating or performance-based agencies in the public sector and entering into formal contracts with these agencies, providing them with greater managerial flexibility while holding them accountable for specified outputs or outcomes.

- In New Zealand, beginning in the early 1980s, commercial and other contestable activities were hived off, corporatised or privatised. The remaining large, multipurpose ministries were split up into business units headed by managers on fixed-term, output-based contracts with considerable autonomy (including the right to hire and fire). These reforms helped to turn a budget deficit equivalent to 9 per cent of GDP into a surplus during the 1980s and cut the unit cost of delivery by more than 20 per cent in some agencies.

Other types of reform rely on more traditional bureaucratic arrangements in the core public sector, emphasising accountability in the use of inputs, meritocratic recruitment and promotion, and creating a public sector ethos building loyalty and improving performance. Also, user participation, client surveys, published benchmarks, and other mechanisms for increasing public involvement are providing external pressures for better service delivery.

Improving policy-making for service delivery involves setting the right balance between flexibility and accountability. For activities that are contestable (i.e. where there is scope for actual or potential competition from various suppliers), easily-specified market mechanisms and contracting out of services can often improve delivery dramatically. But for many other services there is often no substitute for delivery by the core public sector. Here, encouraging public participation and allowing client feedback can exert pressure for better performance.

REASONS FOR CAUTION

Several countries are now emulating these reforms, but what is feasible in New Zealand may be unworkable in many developing countries. Considerable capability and commitment are required to prepare and enforce contracts, especially for outputs which are difficult to specify in the social services. Selection of the most effective mechanism to improve performance depends on both the characteristics of the civil service and the capability of the government to enforce internal and external contracts. Countries which have a weak capability to enforce complex contracts, and weak bureaucratic controls to ensure accountability under more flexible management regimes, need to proceed with caution.

Furthermore, developing countries are restricted in the choices available to them for public service provision by the weakness of the commercial sector and the dominance of the public sector in organised employment. While public management reforms in industrialised countries focus on enhancing citizen choice, most developing countries still face the basic problem of ensuring access to public services.

Thus, despite the important lessons that can be drawn from the successes of recent years in public service reform in many countries, public service managers must be wary of the direct importation of best practice from abroad without due consideration of the national context. It is important to recognise that there is no one single approach that is appropriate to all public service sectors in all countries all the time. Effective service management can be more successfully arrived at by adopting a portfolio of good practices to suit the particular circumstances of different sectors.

A RANGE OF ALTERNATIVES

Given that increasing public service efficiency has ceased to be a purely economic imperative and become more a question of sound governance, public service managers are faced with a new and wider range of alternative methods of service delivery. Taking account of the fact that no single strategy for improving service delivery is likely to be appropriate to all the various areas of public administration, and, looking at service reform from outside a purely ideological or fiscal perspective, it is evident that governments are best served by a range of different strategies through the different sectors of public administration. It is now possible to abandon the notion of a unitary civil service, clearly distinguishable from the private sector.

There has been a paradigm shift which envisages governments dismantling centrally regulated bureaucracies and replacing them with a range of alternative mechanisms of service provision. Governments must consider managing a portfolio of diverse service providers whether they be arms-length agencies, commercial contractors, community groups or national or international voluntary agencies.

- Canada is at the forefront of the movement towards this new paradigm of service delivery, both at a federal and a provincial level. Direct delivery is becoming less viable as a policy instrument. Subsidies and regulations have been eliminated; service providers privatised; responsibility for programme provision devolved to other levels of government, the private sector or the 'community' sector. Partnerships with other sectors of society in order to reduce overlap have resulted in such initiatives as the Canada Business Service Centres which provide one-stop access to information and services.

This pluralistic approach is also perhaps more appropriate to the developing world than previous paradigms of public service delivery. Industrialised countries are now dismantling the unitary, centralised structures developed in the post-war years; structures which developing countries have also sought to establish since independence, but which have suffered through lack of revenue and poor infrastructure. The management of diverse and devolved mechanisms of service delivery, by cutting out the need for costly centralised bureaucracies, provides an opportunity for less-developed nations to leap-frog the era of 'big government' which has proved unsustainable in the developed world. There is a need for caution in adopting new approaches to public service delivery, but there is also significant potential for giving a real boost to the prospects of sustainable development.

THE NEED FOR BALANCE

In designing and delivering government services, a balance must be found among a number of potentially conflicting requirements namely:

- limiting cost to the taxpayer;

- responding to the specific requirements of service recipients;

- supporting national policy objectives; and

- adhering to public values and democratic principles.

In the past, government was primarily concerned with supporting public values and democratic principles and paid less attention to expenditure restraint and responsiveness to client needs. Cost control focused mainly on inputs with little attention paid to service outputs and programmes were expected to support a range of sub-objectives, such as regional distribution, as well as their primary objectives. The result was a common set of procedures and policies that failed to recognise the specific needs of each programme.

The response to this traditional imbalance was to attempt to reduce the cost of government and improve the efficiency of services, as in the example of New Zealand, but this alone, it has been realised, has not reversed the decline of citizens' confidence in public governance. One reason for this is that economic restructuring, while essential, has created many 'losers', denied rightful access to public services, and damaged the trust of citizens in their governments.

There is now a consensus that in-depth review of the role of government in public service provision should precede downsizing. Cost-cutting alone, without attention to role and purpose, tends just to reduce service and cause unexpected damage to public confidence and public servants' morale. There is thus a dilemma involving questions of legitimacy: while citizens do not want to be taxed to have government do things which could be done better by other institutions or enterprises, there are many things which only governments can do, which must be done better, in the fairest, most ethical way.

It is, then, important to recognise the need to keep all four elements in the list above in balance. The nature of this balance (i.e. the relative emphasis placed on each element) should be driven by the nature of the service and the pressures upon it. The result is greater diversity in approaches to service delivery. Governments have come to the realisation that this balance is better respected by managing diverse portfolios of service providers, thereby avoiding the inevitable inequities of a unitary approach to service delivery focused solely on fiscal reduction.

FINDING THE BALANCE

This more open-minded approach, less restricted by the 'new right' political ideology and the fiscal requirements which initially drove public service reform is also in keeping with more recent political thinking. By seeking to manage a portfolio of different approaches to service delivery, governments can be sure that, whilst still concentrating on results and performance, they do not lose sight of their duty to the public good. In this way, fears expressed in the 1980s about 'the death of government,' and concerns over democratic deficit and social exclusion, which have resulted from public sector downsizing and privatisation, can be properly addressed. The experience gained in the first waves of public service reform has made it evident that there are important differences between public and private sectors which must be taken into account by adopting what might be called a 'middle way' in public sector management. This involves:

- working with the private sector but distinguishing the public interest from private gain;

- working with donor agencies but maintaining the integrity of public policy; and

- co-ordinating work with NGOs but without restricting their ability to do their job through over-regulation.

The accommodation of a number of different strategies within a management portfolio also avoids another pitfall of over-emphasising the market-based approach which is that it is based upon assumptions about people and organisations as rational economic actors. These assumptions are problematic since they contradict important cultural values held throughout much of the world. Thus, in many sectors of public service there may be key functions and commitments which only the government itself can fulfill.

Therefore, this new public service management paradigm retains the emphasis of recent decades on results-based and customer-orientated service delivery, whilst avoiding minimalistic government where this might result in social exclusion and a failure to serve the public good.

A CONTINUING PROCESS

The pace of change in the public service, driven by the changing role of governments seeking to respond to a rapidly shifting economic and social environment, will not slacken. Social expectations will continue to rise. Developments in information technology will enable further dramatic organisational restructuring. National competitiveness will increasingly depend on flexibility in highly-skilled work-forces, requiring fast responses from a government that is enabling rather than providing the directions for change. Above all else, fiscal pressures on government budgets at all levels seem likely to continue for many years. Strengthening partnerships of all those involved in service delivery, e.g. politicians, public servants, private sector and non-governmental organisations (NGOs), and seeking to manage a combination of innovative service delivery mechanisms that can contain costs and improve the quality of public services is will continue to be sound public policy.

IMPROVING QUALITY MANAGEMENT

Quality management is the creation of a culture of commitment to identifying and meeting customer requirements throughout whole organisations, within available resources. The approach defines standards for each area of activity, from which performance standards are set for each member of staff and unit of management. Performance is then regularly assessed against customer expectations and satisfaction. Commitment to quality management is openly acknowledged and performance is made public.

The term 'customer' here has a broad meaning: any citizen engaged with government, or any person acting as proxy for the public. For example, New Zealand includes the minister as a proxy customer for the policy advice outputs of the department.

The idea of quality management originated in the private sector, but has become increasingly relevant to government as rising expectations have highlighted areas of unacceptably low standards of service to the public, to officials, and to politicians. Increasingly in Commonwealth countries, the reputation of government is improving through the application of quality management approaches within the public service.

Improvements in quality require improvements in human resource management, with an emphasis on leadership, team-building and performance management; and restructuring, particularly organisational changes leading to flatter pyramids and improved communications.

Singapore's Work Improvement Teams
Singapore was the first public service to introduce Work Improvement Teams (WITS), developed from the Quality Control Circles employed in successful and innovative private sector companies. These teams allow groups of staff of any gradeform the same work area to meet regularly to discuss openly and honestly the obstacles to quality and to devise practical solutions for service improvement. WITS aim to improve performance, motivation and quality of work life. All new entrants to the public service are automatically assigned a WIT. Existing staff who are not members of any WIT either form new teams or are co-opted into existing WITS. A newly-formed WIT will have to complete at least one project within its first year of formation. Subsequently each WIT is expected to complete two or three projects a year. A WITS convention is held every year to recognise outstanding contributions.

Changes in the work culture and systems are encouraging a respect for excellence at all levels. Success within the public sector is recognised and rewarded. Practical and measurable quality standards are set, with participative mechanisms established to ensure that the need for quality has a broad ownership at all levels of staff.

- The Botswana Government introduced the Productivity and Quality Improvement Programme in 1993 by creating Work Improvement Teams within various institutions and departments.

ISO standards for quality management in Malaysia

In Malaysia, the civil service has implemented ISO 9000 at all levels of administration. The implementation of ISO 9000 requires continuous adherence to a comprehensive quality management system that is based on internationally-established quality standards. The elements of the system encompass organisational structure, responsibilities, procedures, processes and resources for implementing quality management. A quality system based on the ISO 9000 standard will ensure that an organisation's products and/or services continuously meet the needs of the customer. A set of guidelines was prepared in 1996 and an action plan for its implementation on a stage-by-stage basis covering the period to the year 2000 has been drawn up.

TRENDS IN MANAGING PUBLIC SERVICES

Although individual countries have emphasised different aspects of managing public services and adopted different approaches to implementation, certain general trends are apparent. Key among these are:

- focusing on the core responsibilities of central government, while devolving non-core activities to local government and non-government organisations (including privatisation);

- reducing costs to taxpayers by improving efficiency, reducing overhead and control costs, eliminating non-productive activities and exploiting opportunities to generate revenue;

- focusing management attention and accountability more on achieving results, in terms of efficiency, effectiveness and quality of service, and less on compliance with detailed rules;

- decentralising authority within government organisations, thus providing delivery units with greater flexibility to achieve results;

- paying increased attention to the service needs of programme recipients, such as easier access, simplified procedures, published standards for service times and more courteous service;

- making greater use of market-type mechanisms, such as direct competition and competitive contracting, to provide incentives and allocate resources;

- working more with other levels of government or the private sector rather than working on its own; and

- the strengthening of strategic capacities at the centre to guide the evolution of the state and allow it to respond to external changes and diverse interests automatically, flexibly, and at least cost; and

- fostering the exchange of public management ideas and experiences within and between governments.

Some of these changes have been implemented to varying degrees in different countries. However, in many cases, they remain more as statements of intent than actual accomplishment. The changes have meant that instead of thinking in terms of processes and rigid frameworks for service provision, institutions and individuals are encouraged to focus more on improving the results of public service interventions, including exploring alternatives to direct public provision.

However, there are possible risks to these changes including:

- under-resourcing of some activities, leading to service deterioration;

- negative impact of staff reduction and changes in human resource management on staff morale and motivation;

- loss of policy cohesion, operational co-ordination and responsiveness to the wishes of the government that may accompany increased autonomy for delivery units;

- undermining of public values, such as fairness, consistency, and probity;

- pursuit of performance targets and service standards that skew performance in ways that do not respond to the broader public interest;

- capture by clients, local/special interest groups, or suppliers/sub-contractors;

- weakening of the potential for policy formulation to benefit from insights gained through operational experience; and

- loss of control over programme costs.

PERFORMANCE MANAGEMENT

A key issue facing managers in all parts of the public service is to demonstrate that resources are being managed economically, efficiently and effectively. In order to demonstrate these achievements at the levels of the individual, team, department and whole organisation, the ability to measure, manage, and report performance is required. Traditionally in the public sector the emphasis was on how money was spent, however the concern now is with the effectiveness of expenditure.

The term "performance management" describes the systematic approach to performance involving a regular management cycle in which:

- performance objectives and targets are determined for programmes (and in many cases made public);

- managers responsible for each programme have the freedom to implement processes to achieve these objectives and targets;

- the actual level of performance against targets is measured and reported;

- the performance level achieved is used in decisions about future programme funding, changes to programme content or design, and the provision of organisational or personal rewards or penalties; and

- the information is also provided to review bodies, such as legislative committees and the external auditor, whose views may also be used in the decisions referred to above.

Performance management systems are key instruments for linking the management of people to organisational goals and strategies. Yet, in many cases they are not used to their full potential.

- The most highly developed system is in New Zealand, where the system of purchase contract agreements between departments and the government makes it imperative that departmental outputs are tightly managed and that the work of employees contributes to the desired outputs. There is a chain of performance agreements, with specified performance targets derived from corporate objectives, from the chief executive downwards through senior management to middle management and staff.

PERFORMANCE MEASUREMENT

For public sector agencies, performance measurement is a major aspect of accountability. Financial reporting alone is insufficient to meet this requirement. While financial reporting covers the collection and distribution of funds and the allocation of resources, it does not show the service provided nor the quality of these services. A set of performance measures is needed to provide a balanced and accurate picture of an organisation's performance.

Performance measurement provides a valuable tool for management. In particular, measurement of performance can assist towards improving the delivery of goods and services. As a result, the best performance measures tend to be those integral to the organisation's business and not merely a set of data prepared to meet an external reporting imperative.

However, performance measurement in the public service poses particular problems. Much public service activity does not lend itself to precise quantification, particularly with regard to quality. Perceptions of quality can vary from client to client. It should be recognised that the achievement of performance measures can be affected by factors beyond the control of the department, such as unexpected delays in other government agencies and changes in government policy.

Performance measurement is compatible with various modern management approaches, such as Total Quality Management. Performance measurement, while focused on operational issues, can also be used to inform a department's strategic planning process. Further, the development of performance measures can be enhanced by an effective management information system.

In evaluating performance levels, it must be recognised that a performance measure is relative, and must be evaluated by reference to some base. While actual performance will be compared to budget or targets, these can be set at tight or achievable levels and, in turn, be based on past performance or performance of other comparable organisations.

BENCHMARKING

Benchmarking is a useful tool to compare the performance between different organisations, or different units within a single organisation, undertaking similar processes. Comparisons can be used to identify, and work towards, best practice and to ensure that managers do not become complacent about current levels of performance. A typical benchmarking process would have the following stages:

PLAN
Design a programme around a key process
↓
MEASURE
Establish the benchmark and current performance
↓
ANALYSE
Find the best practices and identify areas for improvement
↓
IMPLEMENT
Implement best practices

In the public sector, some organisations undertake the same type of work, e.g. courts, hospitals and public libraries. While others may undertake at least some of the same activities, e.g. maintaining buildings, catering and paying staff. At the broadest level, it is possible to compare approaches to customer service, staff management, public relations etc. with organisations – from either the public or private sector – recognised as leaders in the field.

The areas of work which are suitable for benchmarking vary from one organisation to another. However, the first step in benchmarking is to identify the 'core processes', i.e. those activities which, if improved, will have the greatest impact on the organisation's performance.

Each activity selected for benchmarking should be evaluated; the start, content and end points of the activity must be clearly defined, with the factors critical to successful service delivery being specified, and the measures and indicators necessary to report achievement.

The benchmarking process encourages change. By evaluating selected activities and comparing them with similar activities being undertaken elsewhere, the process not only identifies the need for change, but it also identifies what must change and provides a measure of the results that may be achieved.

Benchmarking in the UK Department of Employment

This technique was used in the UK Department of Employment in its Contracts Branch to provide for continuous improvement and direct planned innovation into its operations. The focus initially was on the Contracts Branch's internal operations but later it was extended to all stakeholders in partnership towards continuous improvement of services. Benchmarking was found to be a powerful technique which can reap large benefits if conducted properly. Around 40 departments and agencies are now introducing the process.

- Australia Post has been benchmarking its performance in areas like postal overhead costs and domestic letter costs with six European postal services since 1995. When benchmarking customer satisfaction, the group of postal organisations compared their best practices against two 'best-in-class' companies – Rank Xerox and Ford. This reflected the group's belief that their competition is unlikely to be restricted to postal services and that, despite recent improvements, there was no room for complacency.

IMPROVING HUMAN RESOURCE MANAGEMENT

New approaches to human resource management have been evident over the past decade. These have arisen from a recognition that improvements in the efficiency and effectiveness of the public service are closely linked to such issues as pay and employment practices, working methods, and the performance and attitudes of staff. Increasingly, people are regarded as the principal resource of the public service and managing them well is the key to its ability to cope with new and evolving demands. Good management of the public service involves maintaining this human resource with its competencies and its commitment to act in the public interest.

While the extent and content of reforms in human resource management vary among countries, common features among some developed countries include:

- the devolution of responsibility for human resource management from central bodies to line departments and agencies and to line managers;

- a greater focus on, and new approaches to, the management of senior public servants;

- increased emphasis on training and development and on performance management; and

- the development of more flexible policies and practices in areas such as pay and conditions of employment, classification and grading, staffing, and working arrangements.

Reforms are generally aimed not only at providing managers with more discretion to manage their staff, but also at improving the skills of public servants and strengthening their commitment to quality service and accountability to the public. Often, therefore, increased managerial flexibility is combined with measures such as greater involvement of staff in decisions affecting their work and working conditions, equal employment opportunity policies, and improved career structures. Cost-cutting measures such as pay restraint and efforts to cut public service employment have usually been found to be an element of undermining other human resource management reforms.

Recent innovations in the management of human resources involve managing diversity within a unified system and include developing flexible staffing practices, recognising achievement, developing performance contracts, creating a strong public service ethos, and a determination to minimise corruption.

FLEXIBLE STAFFING AND RECRUITMENT PRACTICES

Open recruitment procedures, with wider recruitment for senior posts, are ensuring that vacancies are filled on the basis of skills and competence, limiting political appointments, and weakening the assumption of a career-based public service with semi-automatic promotion on the basis of time served. At senior levels, low reward, high security positions are being replaced with the exact opposite.

A number of governments have, like that of New Zealand, successfully experimented with developing flexibility in working conditions; moving collective bargaining from the entire public service to the workplace and the application of private sector law to the public sector. Some of the most successful Asian economies recognise the importance of recruiting the most talented people available and improving their skills through constant training. Hong Kong and Singapore carry out aggressive recruitment at entry level, entice high-flyers for further training, and generally pay attractive salaries compared with the private sector.

As the emphasis continues to shift from high security careers, shaped by length of service and seniority, towards shorter-term employment contracts and achievement-oriented promotion, a new cadre of responsive managers is emerging.

This shift away from a career public service has been emphasised by the establishment of Senior Executive Services in Australia and New Zealand, offering appointment contracts, performance measurement, and intra-service mobility. The expectation is that public sector managers, often recruited from the private sector, will have a high level of managerial skills and talent and will be flexible enough to manage effectively in any government agency. Singapore has maintained a systematic focus on efficiency as the sole criterion for retaining or retiring senior public servants. Seniority is not the basis for promotion and many of Singapore's permanent secretaries are comparatively young.

Mobility is increasingly being emphasised within the public service. Encouraging officers to move between departments on promotion or transfer is seen as an effective way of achieving versatility and professionalism within the service. Such mobility also assists with developing career paths and succession planning.

In Australia, the practice of mobility is spreading through middle management and lower levels. Many agencies are increasingly filling middle-management vacancies by external transfer from another agency or department. As a result, the career service is seen as being Australian public service-wide and not just limited to the department joined at career entry.

RECOGNISING ACHIEVEMENT

Incentive packages which ensure that skills and, in particular, personal achievements are recognised and rewarded, are also becoming more widespread.

- The Government of Singapore has made a commitment to pay public servants market rates for their abilities and respon- sibilities in order to attract and retain the talent it needs. As a result, senior public servants earn salaries which are extremely high by international standards.

- The Malaysian public service provides a good example of a successful strategy for giving due recognition to, and appreciation of, agencies and individuals through the series of awards it offers. These awards are also aimed at motivating officers to improve their performance in line with the aim of providing quality services. They include the Public Service Innovation Awards to recognise individuals for practical ideas and implementing them to improve the quality of public service. Another is the Public Service Excellent Service Awards to individuals who have rendered services exceeding expectations and the normal responsibilities of their job.

Malaysia's New Renumeration System

The NRS was established in 1992 to ensure a personnel management system capable of delivering high qulity services. It introduced, amongst others, the following changes:

• recognition of experience and expertise over academic qualifications for certain posts;

• annual salary progression based on individual performance;

• salary increases for each service sector to be differentiated according to the need and importance of the service; and

• additional allowances and benefits, such as paternity leave or club membership.

Civil servants were given the choice of opting for the NRS or not. 99.5% of employees chose the new scheme over the old.

Performance management systems are key instruments for linking the management of people to organisational goals and strategies, but are often under-utilised for this purpose.

Performance review techniques which identify strengths and weaknesses of individual contributions, and personal career planning, are being introduced in performance management strategies which ensure that personal ambitions and aspirations are harnessed towards the overall service of government.

Performance-based compensation systems in the South African Public Service

Performance-based compensation systems have been introduced and are currently utilised to grant special recognition to personnel who have distinguished themselves from their peers through sustained above-average work performance. This is expected to stimulate the initiative of personnel and to encourage them to be more efficient and effective. Components of the system are:

• MERIT AWARD SYSTEM: applicable to all public servants. A cash amount, calculated at either 18 per cent or 10 per cent of basic annual salary, depending on the evaluation of results, can be made to an individual.

• SPECIAL RECOGNITION: by way of either cash payments or commendations can be granted to personnel for suggestions, invention, improvements, etc.

• DEPARTMENTAL-SPECIFIC AWARD SYSTEM: where awards, bonuses or allowances may be granted to persons of exceptional ability, or to those who possess special qualifications utilised to the benefit of the employer and those who have rendered sustained meritorious service over a long period.

- The Canadian Government has made it a policy to inform employees of the results expected of them in the performance of their work; to make them aware of the standards against which their performance will be judged; to provide them with feedback on a continuing basis and periodic formal feedback; and to act on the conclusions of employees' performance reports.

TRAINING

A highly pragmatic approach needs to be adopted to maximise the effectiveness of all levels of staff for improved service delivery. Training and development programmes to ensure competency are increasingly tailored explicitly to the skills needed to support the vision, objectives and strategies of the government. Among the reasons for the continuing emphasis on training programmes are: the need to invest managers with the necessary skills to handle newly-delegated responsibilities; the increasing knowledge and skills required by jobs in the public service; to develop customer orientation and improve standards of service delivery; to adapt to new technology and new working methods; and to address skill shortages. In general, training and development programmes are seen as playing an important role in inculcating new values and bringing about desired cultural change.

In many countries, departments and agencies are encouraged to develop their own programmes so that they can tailor them to their specific needs. The development of managerial skills, especially at senior management level, is given high priority by many public services. This is generally regarded as an area in which central management bodies should take responsibility in order to ensure that all senior managers acquire the leadership and management skills that are considered essential to the success of public service reforms.

- In several countries, such as Australia, New Zealand and the UK, programmes are based on a set of core abilities that senior managers are expected to acquire. The competency-based approach is being developed across the entire Australian public service as a whole by a joint management-union training council as part of the government's national training reform agenda.

Thus, a major initiative of many training and development initiatives is to inculcate values and skills needed to re-orientate the public service and public servants towards the provision of service to clients and concern with service standards.

CHANGING ORGANISATIONAL CULTURE

ACCOUNTABILITY

Strengthening accountability has been rendered all the more important in the context of greater devolution and flexibility. A wide-ranging and controversial debate has arisen about the concept and practice of accountability and the interdependence between the administrative and political system. The issue is who is responsible to whom, for what and when.

Concepts of accountability reflect the overall organisation of, and interfaces between, the political and administrative systems and encompass three perspectives: accountability within the administrative system, accountability at the interface of the administrative and political system, and accountability within the political system.

- Since 1979 the UK Government has used parliamentary Select Committees to investigate the affairs of each government department or agency. These compliment the work of the Public Accounts Committee in scrutinising policy implementation and ensuring probity in the use of public money.

- The New Zealand Government recognised that crucial to enhancing departmental performance as part of civil service reform was the clarification of lines of accountability between the bureaucracy and the political executive. The relationship between ministers and departmental chief executives was singled out as the critical link in the accountability chain. The minister's role is to set the policy agenda, determine priorities, specify desired outcomes and output levels and then monitor the department's performance relative to them. The task of the chief executive was to satisfy these requirements and to take responsibility for any shortcomings in quality or quantity of output.

Efforts to ensure accountability are frustrated, however, by the number of different constituencies the public service is expected to satisfy. More recently, with the emphasis on quality service delivery and effective citizen orientation within the public sector, there has been a shift, in countries such as New Zealand and Canada, away from the traditional compliance with spending authorities to focus on direct accountability for results and performance. Innovations such as customer surveys and public reporting mean that public servants are accountable to their clients as well as management and political bosses.

In 1995, the Government of British Columbia identified three key elements of accountability information:

- *Organisational performance* – are government departments achieving what they set out to achieve at reasonable cost?

- *Financial performance* – is the public service fiscally responsible?

- *Behavioural performance* – Are government affairs conducted in a manner that complies with legislation and expected standards of conduct?

Furthermore, the primary thrust of accountability should not just be to explain what was intended to happen and what actually happened, but also to explain why the results were as they were. In this, what lessons can be learned and, if necessary, changes made for the future.

Many countries try to ensure accountability within the administrative system by developing performance measurement and costing mechanisms with more systematic feedback to the public concerning the cost and quality of services. Difficulty arises when the political level is taken into account. Politicians may be reluctant to set goals precisely enough for success or failure to be accurately assessed. Public reporting exposes poor performance by senior officials, agencies, departments or other institutions, including that caused by corrupt practices.

Another important aspect is ethical accountability reflecting primarily the general principles of right and wrong behaviour according to the norms of society and reflects the overall culture of a public service. The organisational culture is developed through strengthened employee involvement, transparency in the change process, rewards for team work, recognition of individual effort, and consultation with clients and users.

Competitive behaviour, the use of bonuses and performance-related pay, the tactics required to acquire contracts are all areas where 'traditional' values of impartiality and equity may fit poorly with business values of success.

If enhanced accountability is to act as a pressure for performance improvement, it must be matched by enhanced managerial authority. Devolving responsibility to senior managers allows them the financial and procedural latitude necessary to deliver the outputs for which they are held responsible. However, it must be clear to whom they are accountable, when, and for what. Modernising the role of the bureaucracy represents a particular aspect of this necessary devolution to managers or agency chief executives.

The nature of accountability is increasingly affected by the changing relationship between the public sector and the community. There has been a shift towards formalised and specified contractual relationships, capable of being monitored and, where necessary, enforced. While this increased formality enhances accountability by offering rights of redress not previously available, some accountability is increasingly legalistic rather than co-operative.

PUBLIC SERVICE ETHOS

Instilling a public service ethos is more than a series of injunctions, listing attitudes or behaviours which are not allowed. It is a positive climate in which staff identify with the organisational goals and have a willingness to take a longer-term view of responsibilities. The traditional values of the public service emphasise merit, equity, probity, integrity, ethical conduct and political independence. The values of the new culture must also include leadership, quality, productivity and openness. Creating a working culture which incorporates this set of values must involve a strong partnership between management, employees and the public in the change process. It not easy to train public servants in the adoption of new values, but value change is a key factor in improving the quality and efficiency of service delivery.

> **Creating a culture of reform**
>
> Trinidad and Tobago recognised that the critical element for successful implementation of civil service reforms is focusing on the process that will ensure successful change. As a result, the government has developed processes that identify 'Change Sponsors' (usually a cabinet minister) and 'Change Agents* (usually form within the public service) and emphasise that members of the public service organisations should feel a sense of involvement in the process, share the new vision and own the change.

Values also assume a special importance in modern working environments which are less prescribed by rules and regulations. Clearly set out service values can help public servants exercise discretion in decision-making and respond creatively to changing conditions.

- The Australian Public Service (APS) values are now properly articulated within the legislative framework. Employees and agency heads are obliged to ensure that the APS:

    - is apolitical, performing its functions in an impartial and professional manner;

    - is a public service in which employment decisions are based on merit;

    - provides a workplace which is free form discrimination and which recognises the diverse backgrounds of APS employees;

- has the highest ethical standards;

- is accountable for its actions, within the framework of ministerial responsibility, to the Government, the Parliament and the Australian public;

- is responsive to the Government in providing frank, honest, comprehensive, accurate and timely advice and implementing the Government's policies and programmes;

- delivers services fairly, effectively, impartially and courteously to the Australian public;

- has leadership of the highest quality;

- establishes co-operative workplace relations based on consultation and communication;

- provides a fair, flexible, safe and rewarding workplace; and

- focuses on achieving results and managing performance.

Public service reforms are aimed at developing the organisational culture through strengthened employee involvement; clarity of employee responsibilities; transparency in the change process; rewards for teamwork; recognition of individual effort; and consultation with clients and users. These factors can be equally as effective as higher salaries in improving levels of motivation and professionalism within public service.

■ The Malaysian programme for inculcating positive attitudes, including training courses, lectures, explanatory sessions, and provision of reading materials, provides a successful example of a practical approach to the establishment of appropriate values within an increasingly entrepreneurial public sector.

The formal development of codes of ethics within government marks a significant step in moves towards codifying public sector values at a time of rapid change within the culture and practice of the public sector.

MECHANISMS FOR IMPROVING SERVICE DELIVERY

Public service restructuring programmes in recent decades have resulted in the adoption of a number of different mechanisms for the improvement of service provision, most involving competition and market forces to varying degrees. These are outlined below.

FOCUSING ON EFFICIENCY

Since government resources are always under pressure – demand exceeds supply and expectations consistently exceed what can be afforded – there is a continuing requirement to review activities to ensure that resources are used to best effect and that government can demonstrate sound stewardship.

Efficiency programmes comprise both improvement in standards and performance at no higher, and preferably lower, cost. They question whether a task should be undertaken at all, whether it should be undertaken by government directly, or by contractors paid by government, or left to the private sector to consider its commercial viability.

Efficiency Unit in the UK

The Efficiency Unit, created in 1979, reports to the Prime Minister's Adviser on Efficiency and Effectiveness. The role of the Unit is to advise on how to improve the efficiency and effectiveness of central government and to help government departments to improve the value for money of the resource which they use. It does this through an Efficiency Scrutiny Programme. These scrutinies are then publicised within the public service to create a climate of competitiveness and achievement.

Since 1995, departments and agencies have drawn up efficiency plans each year, including what measures they propose to take to stay within their running cost limits for the coming three years. These include privatisation, contracting out and market-testing. The Efficiency Unit, in co-operation with the Treasury, reviews these plans and liaises with departments where necessary.

Under the overall direction of a central co-ordinating unit, such programmes can progressively review the functions of all ministries to ensure that only essential activities are undertaken, and examine whether privatisation of some services would be more efficient. Where there is no strategic reason why an activity should be privatised, corporatisation or contracting out should be considered.

While the Canadian Government has no efficiency unit per se, the Treasury Board Secretatiat has developed two guides for managers which help them determine the most efficient ways of delivering public services. *Stretching the tax dollar: Making the Organisation More Efficient* outlines a five-step process for focusing on the examination of various scenarios for service delivery:

- Preliminary Assessment involves choosing an activity and reviewing the service to define the major issues. If the cost of the study is determined through the preliminary assessment to be greater than the potential savings, the process ends.

- Comprehensive Assessment defines the output specifications of a service, examines various delivery options, reviews the in-house performance of the work and designs a more efficient in-house organisation.

- Reports include the impact of the preferred scenarios and the necessary implementation plans.

- Implementation of the option approved by senior management.

- Monitoring and Review to assess the continues efficiency and relevancy of the service.

DECENTRALISATION

Decentralisation of service delivery – moving resources and responsibilities to lower levels of government – is another potentially powerful means of introducing internal competitive pressure, particularly for the provision of public goods with inter-jurisdictional spill-overs or economies of scale. Local governments get the flexibility to match supply to local preferences or demands, while local accountability and inter-jurisdictional competition in supply provide potential restraints.

The rationale for decentralisation is that power over the production and delivery of goods and services should be handed over to the lowest unit capable of dealing with the associated costs and benefits. In many countries this will involve scaling back the power of central government. Depending on the institutional environment, decentralisation can improve state capability by freeing it to focus on its core functions; it can also, however, undermine that capability.

The appropriate institutional preconditions that need to be in place if decentralisation is to improve efficiency and equity include:

- *Political will* – specifically, consensus that decentralisation constitutes an effective means of increasing local participation and making government more representative.

- *Regular consultation with all major interested parties*, both local and central, on the principles, methods and timing of the process.

- *Administrative commitment* of concerned institutions and their personnel to the success of what in most Commonwealth settings has proved to be a gradual decentralisation programme. Co-operation is required so that new responsibilities are successfully assumed.

- Realism and prudence on the part of *local government* in analysing its capacities and abilities to handle the various tasks to be decentralised.

- Acceptance of *incrementalism*, applying decentralisation features as and when the right conditions are created. Incrementalism can include an asymmetric approach in which reforms are adopted differently in different parts of the country, accepting the need to co-exist with different organisational models according to specific conditions, and relaxing the principle of administrative uniformity.

- Collaboration with local associations and organisations in the implementation of the decentralisation process.

- Sufficient *capacity of the central government* to manage the process, create the conditions for success, and reinforce weak local organisations.

In Commonwealth developing countries, many governments are decentralising responsibilities to regional levels. South Africa is working on a new constitution which favours the provinces. Zimbabwe is decentralising responsibility in areas of health, education and social service welfare to local government.

While in principle, service provision at provincial and regional levels are more sensitive to the needs of local communities, in practice, enhancement of responsibilities depends on the viability and vitality of the local government system and the capacity of local agencies to strengthen social infrastructure and improve access to resources.

Decentralisation mirrors the broader devolution of managerial authority and has been one of the key strategies of reform. Traditional bureaucracies have been characterised by a high level of central control and direction. Increasingly, it is being accepted that managers in public service must be held responsible for results but be allowed to manage. In many countries, such devolution will require legislative and even constitutional changes.

- In Sri Lanka, devolution of powers to eight provincial councils was a major historical landmark in the evolution of political and social institutions. It also provided a unique opportunity to restructure the administration in a manner that would strengthen and enhance democratic policy by the people.

Monitoring arrangements appropriate to the new devolved environment need to be devised by the central bodies to determine how policies for which it is responsible are working in practice. Many countries have found that the shift away from centralised control has resulted in a decline in the quantity and quality of information received by central bodies, thereby impeding effective monitoring. Monitoring systems need to satisfy the centre's legitimate requirements for policy information without infringing the new operational autonomy of line units. The centre can develop incentives for the provision of information by making available both the information it has collected and information it generates itself.

As well as the notion of devolving power, decentralisation incorporates the idea of moving functions away from central government in the geographical sense. The relocation of government departments can also improve efficiency and cut costs.

- UK Government departments are expected regularly to consider relocation to sites offering best value for money, easier labour markets and increased operational efficiency. Since 1988, Departments are required to report to the Treasury each year on their progress with, and plans for, relocation.

> **HMSO**
>
> Her Majesty's Stationary Office, one of the oldest sections of the public service in the UK, founded in 1786, provides printing, publishing and office requisites for the British Government and, in 1988, became an executive agency. Since 1982, other government departments have been free from the requirement to buy all stationary and printing through HMSO, thus providing an incentive to offer a better quality service at competitive prices.
>
> The message that the government does not owe the department its living has been picked up. Managers appreciate that the Agency will only survive as long as the value added by the involvement of an in-house enterprise outweighs any additional cost.

Discontinuation, privatisation and contracting out of an activity should be considered before relocation. If none of these options is practical, relocation is a further possibility.

INTERNAL COMPETITION

Some countries are experimenting with ways to increase competition within the public sector to improve service delivery. Most agencies have traditionally received services such as property and printing from a central body free of charge and have therefore had no incentive to economise in terms of quantity or quality. Recently, several countries have introduced user-charging for these services. As a result, the supply of services is determined by the amount the consuming agencies are prepared to pay.

A number of countries have gone further to create internal markets by allowing the purchase of services from alternative suppliers. The public sector provider must compete directly against the private sector for public sector business.

USER CHARGES AND COST RECOVERY

In many countries, user fees are charged on external customers for services in an attempt to strengthen market signals and thus improve resource allocation decisions in the public sector. User charges are also part of cost-recovery schemes. As for internal markets, the introduction of charging linked with the breaking of monopoly supply can considerably strengthen market discipline. It institutes stronger incentives to control and reduce costs, increase quality and generally be responsive to consumers' needs.

- Client service improved dramatically when the Attorney-General's Legal Practice in Australia moved to user-charging. It now conducts regular surveys of clients and has established client focus groups. This has enabled the Legal Practice to customise its service delivery to the particular needs of clients. The move to user-charging has also had a positive effect on staff. An extensive programme was put in place to upgrade the commercial skills of staff and sustain the cultural change needed to adapt to the new environment.

User-charging can also improve access to public services where governments lack the finances to provide them from tax revenues.

- Willingness to Pay surveys conducted for the Sri Lanka National Water Supply and Drainage Board indicated that among households that did not have existing connections to mains water, ninety per cent were willing to pay for access to the mains supply.

It should also be recognised that charging fees creates a direct accountability relationship with clients of public services. Accountability arrangements ensure that revenue-generating organisations continue to focus on their critical tasks and do not give undue attention to revenue-generating activities. Good public relations and open communication are important to the success of cost-recovery initiatives.

- The Australian Government has introduced user-pays principles to public sector agencies, so that when one part of government needs a service from another, it is increasingly common that it has to pay for it. The purpose of this approach is to make it clear to managers that nothing is free of charge, and to encourage them to modify their behaviour accordingly. Before ordering a service, the manager who has to pay for it will determine whether or not it is essential.

Risks associated with fee-charging include:

- limiting access to services for which fees are charged, which may lead to social exclusion, undermining the 'public good' role of the service;

- encouraging government organisations to focus more on value-added activities and pursuit of markets, e.g. international, that generate revenue rather than on their core responsibilities;

- the introduction of what amounts to an additional tax in cases where fees exceed the costs of providing the service; and

- protection of government monopolies from the need to improve efficiency.

Thus, fee-charging can create pressure to minimise costs and increase responsiveness to client needs, but may also be putting at some risk policy support and maintenance of public values, such as fairness and consistency.

It is crucial, therefore, that in introducing user charges the equity considerations of potential clients are recognised. Reduced charges should be considered for users where full cost recovery would represent an excessive financial burden on individual users. This may be especially relevant to lower-income individuals, smaller entities, users located in remote areas, and heavy volume users of services.

COMMERCIALISATION

At its core, commercialisation allows agencies to act flexibly in response to market signals, even though they may continue in the public sector. Commercialisation entails transparent funding arrangements in which financial 'ring-fencing' identifies all funding inputs, including government subsidies, allowing subsidised and unsubsidised prices to be established for all outputs. It frequently involves vertical restructuring – the separation of interdependent activities previously undertaken within the same organisations. There is also generally a need to change the legal basis of the entity, to establish an organisation which is capable of trading and which can address commercial objectives.

The aim is to develop a market environment that requires management to mimic the behaviour of the competitive firm. This requires, first, that they be given as much independence as possible and be placed at arm's length from departments, ministers and the parliament. They also need clear directions regarding strategic objectives and responsibilities, for which ministers remain politically responsible. Achieving objectives and meeting responsibilities is then left to the management of the enterprise. The process of commercialisation requires separating regulatory functions from service delivery functions.

> **Commercialisation in Namibia**
>
> The Department of Communications has been commercialised with two corporations, namely Namibia Post and Telecom Namibia, freeing them of unnecessary restrictions and enabling them to adopt a more commercial and customer-oriented approach. The Namibian Press Association has also been commercialised and the Communications Commission is now going through the same process. The Namibian Government is also commercialising and privatising the promotion of tourism and wildlife resorts.

A number of countries have favoured privatisation in the interests of ensuring operational independence, reducing the risks of capture by special interest groups, and raising much-needed funds. But the problem of regulatory control remains unresolved where the privatised enterprises have natural monopolies and/or where there is believed to be a large element of 'public interest'. Commercialisation, when properly monitored, can offer the benefits of privatisation without the associate risk.

Competition is the essential catalyst to improved performance. A lesson learned from industrialised countries is that all enterprises, whether public or private, are found to be more efficient when product markets are competitive or contestable. When market forces are allowed to operate in such settings, large efficiency and consumer welfare gains are forthcoming.

ESTABLISHING OPERATING AGENCIES

Traditionally, the primary structural choices facing government concern the height and breadth of departmental bureaucratic pyramids. Accountability is assumed to

Positive use of the public enterprise model in New Zealand

Since 1987, the New Zealand Government has "corporatised" numerous government departments producing goods and services (e.g. electricity generation, forestry and mining) into "State-Owned Enterprises"(SOEs) that operate along commercial lines with a board of directors, accountable to the Minister of Finance, appointed to each. As fully commercial enterprises, they have achieved substantial productivity gains and higher service quality and returned dividends to the government. Government functions are now largely grouped in accordance with a new rationale: trading activities are in the commercial mainstream, policy advice activities are close to the government, and service delivery activities are being aligned more closely with their consumers, under the supervision of management boards. In several cases, corporatisation was accompanied or followed by regulatory reform and privatisation.

In 1991, the key principles governing the operation of SOEs were set out as follows:

- non-commercial functions would be separated from major state trading organisations;

- managers would be required to run them as business enterprises;

- managers would be responsible for using inputs, for pricing, and for marketing their products within performance objectives agreed with ministers;

- the enterprises would be required to operate without competitive advantages or disadvantages, so that commercial criteria could provide a fair assessment of managerial performance; and

- enterprises would be set up on an individual basis depending on their commercial purposes, under the guidance of boards comprising members generally appointed from the private sector.

Later, these principles were altered to require financing of expenditure from market sources and not from government loans, and payment of taxes and dividends.

flow upwards, with the administrative dimension funnelled smoothly towards the Permanent or Chief Secretary, and the political dimension towards the Minister. By contrast, recent experience shows that governments are choosing from a considerably broadened range of structural options. The core public sector has been divided into separate business groups or operating agencies. In general, these agencies have greater managerial flexibility in the allocation of financial and human resources and greater accountability for results.

> **Special Operating Agencies**
>
> In 1989, the Canadian Treasury Board established Special Operating Agencies (SOAs), identified as one of the key initiatives of public service reform. These are service units within departments that are given more direct responsibility for results and increased management flexibility where this is necessary for them to reach new standards in service delivery. The SOAs have the following characteristics:
>
> - they are discrete units of sufficient size to justify special consideration;
>
> - they are concerned with delivery of services rather than with policy advice;
>
> - they are able to be held independently accountable within the parent;
>
> - they are amenable to the development of clear performance contracts;
>
> - they operate under a stable policy framework with clear on-going mandate; and
>
> - they are staffed with managers and employees committed to the SOA goals.
>
> The Canada Communication Group (CCG), one of a number of SOAs within Public Works and Government Services Canada (PWGSC), was one of the first five SOAs to be established and by 1993 already boasted much improved employee moral and performance and a 90% customer-satisfaction rating.

- In the UK, almost two-thirds of the civil service has been moved into executive agencies which have specific service delivery functions. These changes have been accompanied by substantial devolution of managerial authority and accountability for results.

- Among developing countries, Singapore was the first to create focused business units. In the early 1970s, the Singapore civil service adopted the concept of Statutory Boards to achieve specific social development goals. They were designed to counter the traditional public service emphasis on regulation and monitoring, and were structured specifically to encourage the return of talent previously lost to the private sector.

The establishment of operating agencies and the experience of corporatisation in Australia has allowed a clear delineation between the functions of policy formulation and policy implementation. In this way, areas of relative freedom from bureaucratic constraint have been created in which a more business-like climate can be maintained. Establishing an operational unit around a clearly demarcated and coherent set of functions, allows the development of operational goals, uniting staff with a clarified sense of mission.

However, countries with inadequate controls need to proceed with caution. The industrialised countries that have now relaxed detailed control over inputs did so from a position of strength having developed over many years a series of restraints on behaviour that was not credible or accountable. For the many countries that have not yet succeeded in instituting credible controls over the use of inputs, greater managerial flexibility will only increase unaccountable and corrupt behaviour. Furthermore, writing and enforcing contracts, particularly for complex outputs require specialised skills that are often in scarce supply.

While performance contracts have not succeeded in most developing countries, many have sought to create operating or performance-based agencies for easily specified and high priority tasks, such as, tax collection and road maintenance. These agencies are typically set up as free-standing business groups within the civil service, with greater managerial flexibility in the allocation of financial and human resources, better pay, and greater accountability for results. In Africa, operating agencies have been created to achieve tax collection targets in Ghana, Uganda, Zambia. Other countries are likely to follow suit.

In these instances, tax collection through agencies has been considered a prerequisite for boosting a government's capacity to raise revenues and improve incentives for the rest of the civil service. The results have been impressive.

- Ghana was the first country in sub-Saharan Africa to introduce a performance-based approach to tax and customs revenue collection. Total revenues nearly doubled in the first five years, from 6.6 per cent of GDP in 1984 to 12.3 per cent in 1988, largely due to better collection. However, problems arose at the special treatment given to tax collectors and the Ministry of Finance objected to its loss of authority. The programme could not have succeeded without strong support from the top.

Agencies are usually designed to accomplish short-term goals, but they can also create obstacles to deeper institutional reform. Where output is easily specified – tax revenues collected, for example – agencies may be useful as an experimental stage of reform that can be progressively extended, and as a demonstration that reforms can be effective. But it is important that systematic criteria are employed in selecting which agencies to hive off. And although they are a useful first step, agencies cannot substitute for the longer-term institutional reforms needed to create a motivated, capable civil service.

MARKET-TESTING

Market-testing is helping the government to improve the quality and cost-effectiveness of many services. In market-testing, an activity or service currently performed in-house is subjected to fair and open competition so that departments and agencies can achieve the best value for money for the customer and for the taxpayer. Market-testing compares with 'make or buy' decisions in the private sector.

Market-testing involves:

- identifying the scope and nature of the activity to be considered for market-testing, including regrouping them, if appropriate;

- establishing what level of service is necessary;

- identifying baseline costs;

- assessing the market;

- developing a specification and outline contract/service level agreement documents;

- inviting interest from potential suppliers (though this is not a compulsory step – it is possible to go straight to competitive tender);

- selecting a suitable list of bidders;

- calling for bids from the selected participants;

- evaluating competing bids from external providers and the in-house team;

- awarding a contract or service level agreement;

- monitoring the performance and cost of the operation on a continuous basis; and

- re-testing.

There are three principal benefits to be gained from the market-testing process. First, when considering whether to accept an in-house bid or give the work to an outside contractor, the evaluation will look at improvements in the quality of service available from innovative methods of service delivery.

Second, there may be cost savings. Where an activity is market-tested, and an external bid is successful, it is likely to be because that bid offers greater overall long-term value for money than the current method of provision. Where an in-house bid succeeds, the process of opening up that public sector activity to competition in itself often creates opportunities for greater innovation and effectiveness.

Finally, experience suggests that market-testing will lead to raised standards by making expectations explicit. Greater clarity about standards of service and better monitoring of performance against those standards, regardless of whether the work is retained in-house, will improve the quality of service.

According to UK Treasury Guidelines, in establishing a market-testing programme, each department needs to review its activities and identify possible candidates for market-testing, questions to be addressed include:

- Is the function or activity essential? What are the implications of not doing it? Or of doing it in a reduced or combined form elsewhere?

- Can the activity be performed more economically by other means?

- What is the full cost of the level of service currently provided and that which is considered necessary?

- Is the function or activity organisationally discrete?

- What are the working methods, organisation and use of capital assets?

- What use is proposed of existing staff and assets?

Few activities cannot be subject to market-testing, and therefore managers will be required to justify their decision not to market-test activities. From past experience, those activities which offer the greatest scope for contracting out include:

- those that are resource intensive (running costs or capital investment);

- relatively discrete areas;

- specialist and other support services;

- those with fluctuating workloads;

- those subject to quickly changing markets and where it is costly to recruit, train and retain staff; and

- those with a rapidly changing technology requiring expensive investment.

In the case of new services, where there is no in-house operation, there should be a preference for contracting out subject to management or policy requirements and relative value for money.

COMPETITIVE TENDERING

Competitive tendering covers the stages in the market-testing process from developing the specification up to, and including, awarding the contract or service level agreement. All activities included in the specification which are being market-tested would usually be subject to subsequent competitive tendering.

UK Efficiency Unit's role in market-testing

In 1992, the Efficiency Unit acquired responsibility from the Treasury for the overall policy of market-testing; although the responsibility for developing market-testing programmes rests with individual departments as they are best placed to know their own business and to identify which activities are most appropriate to market-testing. The Efficiency Unit also acts in an advisory capacity, encouraging departments to examine market-testing possibilities, and as a clearing-house for best practice to ensure that all departments are equally aware of the prospects and of the practical considerations that they need to address.

Surveys have shown that the introduction of competitive tendering has yielded significant benefits in the provision of public services. The effect of competition on costs and prices is unambiguous and the weight of evidence indicates that substantial savings are typically achieved, in the order of 20 per cent.

- In Australia, the McCarrey Commission estimated that competitive tendering had the potential to save about $250 million (or 20.3 per cent of the total cost of these functions) from 34 selected government functions in Western Australia. The evidence on quality is less clear cut and its interpretation is made more difficult by data problems.

The main problems with tendering processes associated with the delivery of public services are that they are cumbersome, time-consuming and inefficient; and in some situations there may not be multiple, qualified, private sector providers aware of, and willing and able to participate in a competitive selection process. The process also opens up the possibility of cartel formation after abolition of in-house providers, and the problem of fixed wage costs even after staff transfers.

> **Australia's Job Network**
>
> In 1997-98, Australia's Department of Education, Training and Youth Affairs undertook the largest competitive tendering exercise of its kind in Australia. Organisations within the private, community and public sectors were invited to tender for the provision of a range of services to unemployed people. This resulted in the creation of Job Network – a national network of more than 300 different organisations which specialise in finding jobs for people, particularly the long-term unemployed. The successor to the old Commonwealth Employment Service is now exposed to full and open competition on the same basis as other tenderers. This new market provides the means to tap into the expertise of the private and community sectors to deliver improvements in efficiently, innovation, quality and choice. Contractors are paid primarily on a fee for employment outcome basis, ensuring that the reforms genuinely make a difference to those in need.

CONTRACTING OUT

Contracting out, which follows competitive tendering, is the purchasing of a service from an outside organisation and can be as a result of a market-test involving an in-house bid or a strategic decision to obtain the service from the private sector. The contract becomes the instrument through which relations between the parties are managed and regulated. Contracting-out may also be described as operational privatisation.

Competitive tendering and contracting are considered to be most attractive in the following conditions:

- where competition exists and contracts are usually determined by price;

- where markets have a clear capacity to provide a service;

- where activities are subject to wide fluctuations in workloads or market conditions;

- where agencies do not possess "in-house" capabilities; and

- where functions are new, discrete, or non-core activities.

Contracting out has been well tested within government. Although specialist services (e.g. maintenance, security services, catering etc.) have always been purchased from the private and non-government sectors, it is the development of market-testing techniques which is providing the strategy for assessing the ability of the market to provide goods or services historically considered to lie at the core of government.

The following activities are now commonly bought in:

- Audio-visual services
- Building maintenance
- Catering
- Cleaning services
- Construction
- Courier services
- IT management
- Estate management
- Payroll management
- Personnel management
- Publicity and marketing
- Research and development
- Security guarding
- Social services
- Market research and consumer surveys
- Travel and Transportation

Significantly, market-testing is showing considerable potential as a technique for stimulating change through the assessment of internal efficiency. In a limited number of situations, where contracting out is not feasible because of market weaknesses or political restrictions, the development of internal markets is being explored with, as yet, uncertain results.

Flexibility and a concern for service quality and sustainability, rather than preconceptions concerning the efficiency of the private sector, have been the key features of successful initiatives.

- In the UK, government policy as given in the White Paper *Competing for Quality* considers that the widest possible range of activities should be subject to competition. Targets for market-testing have been set for ministries and agencies and officials are appointed with clear overall responsibility for each organisation's market-testing programme.

- In Australia, the Industry Commission's report on competitive tendering and contracting argues that "competitive tendering and contracting can lead to significant improvements in accountability, quality, and cost-effectiveness, providing benefits to clients, taxpayers, and the broader community", and "is an under-utilised option for improving government throughout Australia".

Monitoring service contracts raises two important areas of concern. First, contracting arrangements have often been associated with a decline in evaluating programme outcomes; and a second area of concern is the measurement of performance. Contract arrangements have mostly been concerned with the cost of providing a service and the number of service units provided. Assessing client outcomes and the quality of services has often been avoided because of both political and technical difficulties associated with this type of analysis.

- In the UK, a study of privately-owned residential homes for the elderly highlighted the incapacity of competitive markets to ensure accountability and monitor implementation. The capacity of markets to monitor programmes depends on the capacity of consumers to articulate demands and assert their interests. However, by definition those are the very attributes consumers of care services are likely to lack. Market mechanisms were considered to be particularly imperfect in situations where proprietors were able to persuade, influence or even intimidate their clients.

While there is general agreement that contracting out is not always appropriate, country experience has provided differing results. Organisations are generally reluctant to contract out sensitive or strategic functions and in any contracting out situation, ensure that critical decisions remain the sole responsibility of in-house staff. The final choice as to whether and what to contract out is a matter for ministers and delegated officials after assessment of the appropriateness in each case. Nevertheless, it is clear that to achieve its full potential, contracting out needs powerful support from the centre.

SERVICE LEVEL AGREEMENTS

If market-testing the in-house bid indicates that it would represent better long-term value for money to keep the service in-house, departments and agencies should proceed with:

- *negotiation* with the in-house team;

- *award* of service-level agreement to the in-house team;

- *implementing* management changes and monitoring the in-house team's changes to the new agreed working practices reflecting the new customer/supplier relationship; and

- *monitoring* performance and cost of the activity against the service level agreement.

DIVESTITURE

Market-testing and client surveys may ultimately reveal that the public would be better served if the full responsibility for the provision of certain services were handed over to the private sector. Although historically conceived as a revenue-raising initiative, it has become clear that, for certain services, the selling off of public companies results in significant benefits for the consumer. The role and contribution of privatisation will vary between countries and across time, according to economic objectives, political imperatives and institutional and structural constraints.

The Balanced Scorecard

The Australian Taxation Office is beginning to use the Balanced Scorecard to measure performance in its service Level agreements between Corporate Service and each programme and policy unit. A Scorecard is a method of measuring service delivery based on both qualitative and quantitative measures. It supplements traditional financial indicators with information on three additional perspectives of organisational performance: customer satisfaction, operational processes, innovation and learning.

Divestiture is achieved by three alternative methods:

- public flotation;

- private sale; and

- management buy-out.

There are a number of steps which need to be taken in order to ensure a successful divestiture. Most importantly, this divestiture should be supervised by a strong central authority responsible specifically for the privatisation process.

- The National Investment Bank of Jamaica is an example of such an agency. It undertakes the following tasks in preparing a divestiture:

    - Financial review of the enterprise.

    - Identification of means of removing impediments to divestiture.

    - Valuation.

    - Recommendation of an appropriate method of divestiture.

    - Invitation of bids through advertisement.

- Screening of prospective investors.

- Negotiations with short-listed applicants.

- Final recommendation to cabinet for approval.

- Supervision of legal arrangements in order to complete the transaction.

However, privatisation can be extremely difficult to achieve and can carry significant social costs, not just as a result of the job losses normally associated with the transfer to the private sector, but also because the company will cease to have any obligation to serving all sections of the public as citizens and will deal instead only with customers. Therefore, plans for privatisation often encounter considerable resistance from labour unions and management in state-owned companies alike.

- Both Sri Lanka and India have experienced such obstacles to the privatisation process, but Nigeria has gone some way to overcoming them by implementing the following measures.

- A code of conduct which prevents members of the privatisation committee and their families from buying the shares or assets of the companies they are responsible for privatising.

- Encouraging transparency by disclosing information on the implementation of the programme to the general public.

- Public awareness campaigns designed to encourage mass participation.

- Deliberately allotting shares sold by the public share offer in favour of the lower income groups.

Two major economic factors are seen as crucial if the privatisation process is to be effective in improving levels of service and efficiency:

- The enterprise should be divested into an open, competitive market. If privatisation simply converts a public monopoly into a private monopoly, the improvement is unlikely to occur.

- Overall macro-economic conditions and policy frameworks should be 'market-friendly.'

Furthermore, it should be noted that certain costs may arise from the difficulties of measuring and controlling the performance and service quality of privatised entities. For example, many countries rely on private companies for waste disposal. It is extremely difficult for governments to ensure that waste products are being disposed of safely by the privatised companies as they tend to resist government attempts to monitor their practices. It therefore requires strong commitment form the government to regulate in this domain.

It is also as a result of complications such as these that the role of divestiture in public sector reform has come to be reassessed. Privatisation can be a very helpful short-term mechanism for raising government revenue, but its value in terms of standards of service provision is not always clear. Its value in best practice terms has depreciated now that it has ceased to be fashionable to see the ideal government as a minimalistic one.

PARTNERSHIP WITH THE PRIVATE SECTOR

Given the risks of privatisation, and the impossibility of implementing privatisation successfully in countries which lack a sufficiently market-orientated macro-economic structure, governments are looking for alternative methods of exploiting the expertise available in the private sector for better service provision. One such alternative is to seek mutually beneficial partnerships with private companies.

The South Bristol Learning Network

This is a good example of how a computer firm, in this case ICL, can improve services in a disadvantaged community by working in partnership with local government in the UK. ICL hired a diverse group of 50 unemployed people, trained them, and they in turn trained their communities in the use of IT. After three and a half years, 15,000 people had been trained. Local teachers and students also participated in the scheme as computers in their school were outdated. The schools benefited from a marked improvement in student behaviour, attendance and performance.

The project has not made any immediate profits for ICL, but the company sees it as a long-term investment in building IT literacy and the market for its services.

Partnership with private enterprise can offer the following advantages:

- *Access to specialist skills.* It is neither practicable nor cost-effective for the government to employ full-time specialists in every conceivable field when individuals from the private sector are willing to take on consultancy when needed.

- *Opportunities to meet demands beyond current government capacity.* When a government does not want to add to its permanent staff or it cannot build up its capacity quickly enough, it may turn to the private sector.

- *Providing clients with more choice of providers and levels of service.* Some alternative service delivery approaches allow clients more choice regarding provider, location, and particular service characteristics. Clients usually have much more limited options if the service is provided only by public facilities.

- *Reduced costs.*

PARTNERSHIP WITH NGOS

The development of partnerships with non-governmental organisations and the private sector has emerged as a key element in implementing some development policies and programmes. In the developing world, NGOs will be major service-providers within the government-managed portfolio.

NGOs can be both partners and competitors in the delivery of public services. When backed by public support, they can exert useful pressure on government to improve the delivery and quality of public services.

- The Grameen Bank in Bangladesh has effectively developed programmes that target services to poor sectors of society.

In most developing countries, NGOs engaged in service delivery are small in scale, working in communities and settings where the reach of government or private providers is weak or non-existent. In Africa, NGOs are the main providers of health care. The importance of these NGOs reflects their ability to substitute for weak public sector capacity and to mobilise funds from a range of different sources, including national and international organisations.

Even though outputs are difficult to specify, governments have contracted NGOs where they are committed to high quality or where, because of their religious or ideological orientation, they can better service certain groups.

- The Government of Uganda is forming partnerships with NGOs to deliver both preventive and curative health services previously in the public domain.

In Asia, co-operative organisations, trade unions, women's and youth clubs, and religious groups are all involved in some aspects of public service provision. Non-governmental and religious organisations provide health, education and training programmes that supplement those offered by governments. In Africa, for example, religious groups have played an important role in supplementing the health system by running hospitals and health clinics and providing social services that are either not available from the government or are inadequate.

- In India, the Government registers and assists housing co-operative societies that buy land and obtain financing for the construction of low-cost housing for their members. Housing co-operatives may account for one quarter of all private formal housing construction in urban areas in India.

Partnership with NGOs creates new management problems for governments. For instance, how can governments manage a credible budget process when many of the resources to be deployed are not in their control? How can governments supervise the national interest, without being drawn into the trap of either micro-management from the centre or intruding on the rights of partner organisations over their own resources? Co-funding, special tax status and review mechanisms are preferable to over-restrictive legislation on these matters.

The involvement of NGOs need not, though, be solely at arms-length level. Strategic intervention by government public service managers can be effective in creating the sort of employment opportunities normally only associated with the private sector. In partnership with NGOs, government can help mobilise local people for social causes by enlarging service delivery. Programmes for sustainable development, such as the Grameen Bank in Bangladesh, normally emphasise schemes for self-employment, but it is also possible to create public service entrepreneurs within the networks provided by NGOs and community organisations. Prudently distributed government grants can facilitate the mobilisation of service delivery at grassroots level.

THE ROLE OF INFORMATION TECHNOLOGY IN IMPROVING SERVICE DELIVERY

In the past two decades, the coincidence of public sector reforms with the much-heralded dawn of the 'Information Age' has meant that government departments have become major users of computers and information management systems. While there are disparities in the extent of investment in information technology (IT) in the public service between countries, broad patterns are evident.

Major improvements have been achieved concerning productivity, and technological and financial considerations (revenue collection, financial management and accounting, and inter-departmental communication systems). These are usually prioritised in the light of financial constraints and impending implementation deadlines. The traditional Anglo-American view of IT use in the public sector has emphasised its potential for rationalising tasks and cost-cutting.

Public sector managers have, in the past, focused IT development on improving efficiency in internal procedures and the 'back office.' More recently, though, IT has come to be seen as a tool that can also improve the quality of service delivery in the 'front office.' IT can reap wider benefits for society than simply reduced costs and government has a duty to unlock this potential.

As governments review the last twenty years or so of public sector restructuring, decentralisation and downsizing, it has also been recognised that the development of IT-use is consistent with the attempt to establish 'joined-up government' – closer integration and liaison between different government businesses whilst retaining departmental autonomy – amidst a climate of devolution. IT can offer the various departments and agencies involved in public service provision the chance for both more effective communication between each other, and more integrated interfacing with customers.

Furthermore, as citizens experience the benefits of technology in other areas of their lives, there is a growing expectation that government services will be provided in similarly flexible and innovative ways. Fears that the information age would create more paternalistic and intrusive government, distempering citizens, have proved wholly misguided. IT is anti-hierarchical by nature, and is increasing the power of individual citizens to access and influence government operations and raise their expectations of public service delivery.

Important factors that are needed to achieve maximum benefits from IT systems include:

- enhanced management, planning and control of the IT function;

- using technology to redesign and improve administrative processes;

- providing better access to quality information;

- harnessing the potential of new technologies;

- developing and applying standards;

- attracting and retaining high calibre IT professional staff;

- increasing research into the economic, social, legal and political implications of new IT opportunities; and

- assessing experiences.

In recent years, the introduction of IT has typically involved a strategic planning process in which organisational objectives are clarified and prioritised. This has been a useful contribution in its own right to organisational effectiveness. IT has also facilitated access by policy-makers to timely and comprehensive information, through better communication systems and the generation of policy-relevant information from operations. This has become all the more crucial in an environment of devolution and separation of policy-making and executive functions.

INNOVATIONS IN SERVICE DELIVERY

As leading private corporations are beginning to use IT to offer services that are simultaneously flexible, accessible, convenient, fast and efficient, citizens, aware of these new service possibilities, are losing their tolerance for traditional 'bureaucratic' service. If, for example, banks are able to offer 24-hour telephone or Internet service, customers begin to wonder why tax offices cannot do the same. Governments are being forced to match the private sector in technological innovation.

'One-stop' services

Leading the field in this area of service delivery are the Ontario Government's ServiceOntario electronic kiosks, which are heavily-used after normal office hours. These were built for the government by IBM which receives a fee of $1 per transaction.

Since 1990, Singaporeans have had access to multimedia interactive information kiosks via the SingaTOUCH network which is used by the government to both disseminate policies and deliver services.

IT has been central to several initiatives to improve access to information and services outside normal office hours, in locations which best suit the client and in multiple forms (different languages, touch screen interrogation, etc.).

- The Australian Taxation Office has developed a system whereby taxpayers will be able to download return preparation software over the Internet, complete their return, digitally sign, encrypt it and then lodge it with ATO also over the Internet.

Moreover, information and services are beginning to be provided to individual citizens via kiosks situated in shopping centres, community centres and other public places. Some developments bring together a wide range of information from many central and local government departments. Others provide both information and services, such as job-seeking and vehicle licence renewal, with the facility for payment by credit card. There are also initiatives that combine public and private sector information.

IT has also supported efforts to provide an integrated service based on the 'whole person' concept rather than on administrative function with the result that, for example, all tax or social security matters relevant to a particular client are dealt with by a single office rather than by different offices. This system has advantages for both administration and client. For the administration, it improves efficiency (by eliminating duplication), control (against fraud and evasion), and effectiveness (by increasing tax inflow or better targeting of service). For clients, it reduces intrusion and compliance costs. But it requires major changes in work practices, communications, organisational structures and computer systems. Although many countries are committed to the approach, implementation has been generally slow, due mainly to organisational barriers between departments or agencies and local levels of government, and the attitudes of civil servants.

> **Telecommunications networking among government agencies in Malaysia**
>
> Malaysia has established the Government Integrated Telecommunications Network (GITN). The project provides a telecommunications infrastructure that is capable of supporting an integrated network of the various government agencies. The network carries a number of applications more cheaply without each individual agency having to worry about maintenance and technical issues. In 1996, a GITN pilot project was initiated which included such applications as video-conferencing and discussion databases.

Many countries are also developing more interactive and easy-to-use systems that enable point-of-contact officials to provide relevant information and service to clients. Many front-line offices now have immediate access to main databases storing information on clients and providing opportunities to establish their entitlements and ultimately to customise the service to their needs within defined limits of discretion. Access to computerised information, greater use of existing information and greater integration or connection among systems are reducing form-filling and enabling speedier, more reliable responses to clients.

PLANNING AND MANAGEMENT OF INFORMATION TECHNOLOGY SYSTEMS

The crucial importance of IT in improving public service provision now means that public sector managers are obliged to view information as a fourth major resource and practice systematic information resource management, ensuring that the right information is reaching the right employee or client at the right time and in the right form.

Many governments have developed policy frameworks which provide a public service-wide focus for effective planning and management of information systems, technology, and organisational engineering involving information technology. These frameworks require clear co-ordination and identify lead agencies capable of tracking fast-moving developments in technology and systems. In some countries, units have been established to promote the use of computers and information technology.

- The Government of Bangladesh has established an autonomous body called the Bangladesh Computer Council (BCC). The major role of the BCC is to assist the government in formulating, co-ordinating and implementing IT-related polices and setting up a framework within public and private sector institutions in order to enable them to collaborate to develop new technologies in Bangladesh.

- In 1994, the Canadian Government released a blueprint paper suggesting ways for renewing government services using IT. It outlined a number of key work principles for redesigning delivery processes:

    - *Single Window/Seamless Service* – services to be delivered through a single window;

    - *Streamlining* – the process between client and service delivery to be minimised;

    - *Choices* – cost permitting – clients to be offered the choice as to how service is delivered;

- *Consistency* – the same type of work activities to be conducted in the same way for different services;

- *Location and Time Independence* – clients to have access to services at any time and from many places, where practicable;

- *Continuous Improvement of Service* – measurements embedded in the service processes to ensure that improvement is continuous.

Effective planning of IT initiatives is also essential if public services are to attract the personnel able to administer new programmes. There is a world-wide shortage of trained IT personnel and governments must compete with the private sector which usually offers higher salaries.

- South Africa aims to create a State Information Technology Agency in order to address the problem of recruiting skilled IT personnel. The proposal is to create a state-owned company which will provide IT services to the rest of the government on a cost-recovery basis, using the services of the private sector where appropriate.

Experience in the UK supports a strategic approach to IT management where departments identify and prioritise group elements for information systems and ensure compatibility with other existing and planned systems. This benefits the approving authority by providing a backdrop against which to consider each proposal for expenditure.

The following is a selection of the specific benefits of a centrally co-ordinated IT policy noted in Singapore, but equally applicable elsewhere:

- improved co-ordination between government departments in the packaging and integration of IT, enabling a synergistic approach towards improving public service;

- better identification and initiation of useful strategic applications that improve service provision;

- the possibility of collective bargaining with information delivery service operators for favourable terms and competitive charges;

- quality-assured products and services;

- enhanced product and service development;

- more accurate monitoring of public acceptance and market need for products and services;

- Ease of technology transfer between departments;

- No duplication of set-up costs.

A properly integrated approach also creates certain additional benefits to the extent that, in the case of the UK and Canada, the exchange of ideas and customised software between government departments has led to the development of skills and products that are sufficiently competitive to be marketed to other governments and institutions, and to the private sector at home and abroad.

Integrated Information Systems

The UK's GCTA or Government Centre for Information Systems is responsible for promoting business effectiveness and efficiency in government through the use of IT. It provides specific services to government departments and agencies, such as helping them plan their spending on information systems and advising them on the best use of their information technology by evaluating various systems available against needs and value for money. While its customers are chiefly government departments and executive agencies, its business environment is wider and includes European and other national governments, European Community institutions, the academic world and the IT supply and service industry.

The Canadian Government's Software Exchange Service (SES) aims to reduce government expenditure by encouraging the sharing of a large inventory of government-owned applications service; fostering an environment for sharing ideas on IT; open opportunities for the private sector to provide software customisation, installation and maintenance services; and identify commercially-marketable government-owned software for licensing. It is estimated that this inter-departmental and inter-regional co-operation saves the government more than $30m annually.

APPLICATIONS FOR EFFICIENCY AND QUALITY

As has been noted in some cases already, IT applications, particularly when taking advantage of networking opportunities between departments and reducing administrative burdens on clients, are achieving significant efficiency savings for the public service. The use of electronic mail, smart cards, electronic data interchange and so forth can dramatically reduce the amount of paperwork required in both intra-governmental business and citizen-to-government business. The significance of computerised databases which can be shared between government agencies is clear when one considers that particulars citizens are required to communicate to, say, vehicle licensing authorities, the police and the tax office. A straightforward change of address need no longer involve the completion of different forms for each section of the public service.

In many Commonwealth countries, the use of information technology has been undertaken with the aim of replacing existing manual systems through a major office automation programme. Computerised text processing, information storage and retrieval, and communication systems have been introduced to increase efficiency and enhance productivity. More recently, countries have been investing in the development of electronic data exchange and generally conducting business electronically wherever possible, such as in the area of procurement. There is also interest in using IT to improve the management and access to regulation.

- Computerisation has made extensive inroads in the Singapore Civil Service and has enabled it to improve efficiency by reducing manpower costs. The Singapore Civil Service Programme has generated S$2.71 in return for every dollar spent on computerisation.

- In Malta, one of the key parameters of the strategic plan for public service reform is based on maximising the information resource through the sharing of information, within the confines of Malta's legislation, to avoid duplication in information collection and maintenance. In order to achieve this, the Government has established an open client-saver architecture platform that allows seamless access of applications systems from a single workstation, with appropriate security safeguards. This input of technology has been very significant in a relatively short space of time, with applications systems in place, or in the course of development, in most major areas of government.

Towards a 'paperless' civil service

The Malaysian Government's objective is to move towards an era of 'paperless' bureaucracy. A network is being established that will enable government agencies to offer their counter services on-line to the public using the computer and network facilities of the post offices. It is hoped that this network will support the provision of 'one-stop/non-stop' services when used along with multipurpose cards for each citizen which will access a variety of government services. These services would include registration of births and marriages; driving licences; and the payment of taxes and pension contributions

The Canadian Government recently announced a blueprint for renewing government services through the use of information technology and thereby bringing services to clients and providing them with 'single-window' accesses for multiple services.

REASONS FOR CAUTION

While successful applications of IT have been evident, there have also been many disappointments and failures. IT investments have not always provided the best value for money or delivered all the expected benefits. The uneven use of IT can also increase external inefficiency and administrative burden. Thus, governments can add to the costs of businesses by not keeping up with their IT investments or by imposing different technical and information standards. A balance needs to be struck between tailoring administrative acts to the needs of individual clients and adding overall complexity, and maintaining uniformity and relative simplicity and transparency.

Technology transfer has long been identified as a key factor within the development process, but a number of problems have been identified in schemes for computerisation in the developing world. First, effective use of IT involves more than simply purchasing the equipment: a number of infrastructure requirements, technical and managerial skills are needed in order to operate it. Second, technologies developed in the West may incorporate particular social and cultural assumptions not applicable elsewhere, such as the value of formal information or legislative stability in the business environment. Thirdly, once the appropriate technology has been obtained from the chosen provider, the donor/vendor may have little interest in making sure that the technology works.

Relevant to even the most technologically advanced of the industrialised nations is the issue of social exclusion raised by the increasing use of IT in public service provision. There is concern that not only are the elderly unable to adapt to new technologies, but the poor, while willing to learn, will remain unable to afford access. The public administration has a duty to ensure that in the race to modernise it does not cut off or marginalise from service provision those on the fringes of society.

Factors such as these emphasise the need for prudent assessment of the potential advantages and costs of investing in IT projects. It has become apparent that many IT investments have been made in a climate of media hype about the miracles of new technology without proper assessment of the real effects on performance or a comprehension of IT's socio-cultural effects within an organisation. As is the case for the other mechanisms for improving service delivery cited here, careful consideration of local circumstances, and the duty of the public administration to serve the public good above all, ought to moderate the outright importation of best practices.

CITIZEN ORIENTATION

As a result of recent changes within the public service, there is a desire in many countries to orient public services, like those produced in the private sector, towards the needs of service-users. This change in emphasis has been due in part to a conscious reshaping of the work culture to achieve a customer or client orientation. Courtesy campaigns, customer-care training, and comprehensive complaints procedures ensure that service-users are seen as active, freely-choosing customers rather than passive recipients of monopolistically-provided state services.

Customer orientation is an area in which it is difficult to generalise at national level. Independent local governments have been using a variety of experiments with customer orientation over services in many countries. Not all the experiments involve the use of market mechanisms but include a variety of forms of consultation and participation in decision-making. These efforts to improve service have been complemented by the development of avenues of redress.

SETTING SERVICE STANDARDS

In some countries, there are initiatives to develop a customer-oriented culture for public service delivery by establishing service standards and evaluating performance based on measures of productivity and service quality.

- Australia's FMIP Performance Information and Management Cycle requires agencies to develop standards to monitor service quality systematically and publish evaluation results.

- Canada's Public Service 2000 Budget initiative requires departments to develop and publish service standards, but these must be fiscally neutral.

> **Example of the Negeri Sembilan Water Supply Department in Malaysia**
>
> As part of its customer focus, the Negeri Sembilan Water Supply Department in Malaysia has introduced the slogan 'Courtesy to the public'. The Customer Service Unit has introduced mechanisms such as radio sessions, meet-the-people sessions, and one-day seminars to gather feedback and at the same time disseminate information to members of the public. Other facilities introduced include mobile counter services or appointing agents to act on behalf of the Department in remote locations, putting up billboards to inform the public on the availability of the hotline service, and the distribution of pamphlets on the Department's activities.

The introduction of Citizen's or Client's Charters signify the commitment of governments, like those of the UK and Malaysia, to the provision of services and outputs to its customers according to set quality guidelines. Schemes such as these recognise that it is the point of interface with a citizen, business or organisation which is most crucial in formulating public perceptions of government services. Images and attitudes are based on direct experiences of service delivery at the point of contact with public servants, waiting in line to post a letter, for example. Therefore, by improving client orientation at these levels, significant changes in public perception can be achieved, even for those functions which remain within the core public sector.

The UK Citizen's Charter

The principles of customer orientation as defined in the UK Citizen's Charter and similar initiatives can be set out as:

- Setting and publicising standards for the services that individual users and private sector firms and other organisations that use public services, can reasonably expect.

- Providing full, accurate information about how services are run, what they cost, how well they perform, and who is in charge.

- The public sector should offer choice wherever practicable and systematic consultation with users of services to determine priorities for service improvements.

- Front-line staff should offer a courteous and helpful service, wearing name-badges and providing convenient opening hours.

- Service-users should have access to an easy-to-use complaints procedure; and if the service has been defective, they should receive an apology, a full explanation and swift and effective redress.

The Citizen's Charter has resulted in more privatisation and contracting out, wider competition and more rigorous and independent inspectorates.

In addition, the UK Government organises the 'Chartermark' scheme which is an award for excellence in delivering public services. Organisations applying must demonstrate the extent to which they have adopted the principles of public service set out in the Citizens' Charter. A charter mark means an organisation has shown that it puts its users first. In 1993, 93 awards given under the scheme were presented by the Prime Minister to public organisations providing services in the following fields: health, local government, privatised utilities, agencies/central government and a small group of 'other' services. In the same year, the Malaysia Government introduced an award for the best formulated Client's Charter.

While market-type reforms are based on the service-user as a 'customer', there is also a concern for the role of citizenship and rights to influence policy and decision-making.

- In Australia, improved client services has been a significant part of the government's reform programme. The Government and ministers decide on what kind and level of services should be provided, on the basis of assessments of the needs and interests of client groups. It is the responsibility of the Public Service and its staff to see that the services desired by the government are delivered effectively, efficiently and in a timely fashion, with proper courtesy and sensitivity and with full regard to the legal rights and entitlements of clients. For the Public Service, this is the nub of client focus and service quality.

Customer Service in the UK Passport Agency

Traditionally an area of the Civil Service that was criticised for its slow and uncommunicative service, the former Passport Office has been transformed since gaining Agency status in 1991. Customers now receive passports within 20 days at peak times of business, 10 days at other times. These are targets set and published by the Agency itself. The Agency also conducts regular surveys of customer opinion. All staff in contact with the public now wear name badges and standard clothing and receive comprehensive customer-care training. Special facilities have been established as part of the Agency's commitment to meet the needs of customers with disabilities.

INTERNALLY-FOCUSED APPROACH

Some administrations have adopted an approach to customer service that is essentially internally-focused. The service providers define service standards, publicise them, and then try to implement and deliver the standards. The customers are not involved in the choice of criteria or in setting the expected standards, but do have a right of redress or compensation if the published standards are not met.

IMPROVING ACCESSIBILITY AND PARTICIPATION

One aspect of citizen orientation is the attempt to make existing services more accessible by the relocation of offices nearer clusters of client populations, the use of alternative delivery mechanisms, the use of information technology, and more convenient opening hours.

Some country programmes provide a single access point to a range of services. This 'one-stop shop' idea has been implemented in many places, including the

Ministry of Industry, Mauritius, and UK local government. However, from the customer's viewpoint, the 'one-stop shop' rarely includes services provided by more than one level of government; municipalities may organise access to all their services in one place, but the customer still has to travel to access the services from the regional or federal level.

Along with improved accessibility, many administrations are trying to simplify procedures to make them more comprehensible to the customers, using plain language and eliminating jargon and codes. Forms are redesigned and simplified, procedures are explained, and staff are trained to make services more user-friendly.

> **The Blue Pages**
>
> It is estimated that in the United States the public consults telephone directories at least 80 million times each year to find the phone number of a government organisation. There are over 6,000 directories which list government numbers in different ways and tend to focus on organisational structures which do not necessarily respond to citizen's needs. 'The Blue Pages Project' is radically changing the presentation of phone numbers, organising information around functions and services provided, publishing Internet and electronic mail addresses and fax numbers. This format is to be applied consistently throughout the country.

MEASURING CLIENT SATISFACTION

The active participation of clients is another key objective. Citizens' participation helps to ensure that the administration takes account of their needs, and fosters a sense of joint responsibility for outcomes. Government organisations must find out what services clients need and how well existing services fare. For this, consultative mechanisms need to be strengthened. Many organisations now make greater use of client surveys, public hearings, and meetings with interest groups, and have welcomed input from the public.

- The Canadian Treasury Board publishes a guide to public service managers of how best to measure client satisfaction. It points out that citizens have concerns which are both direct (courtesy of staff, prompt service, clear forms and signs, etc.) and indirect (fairness and equity, health and safety, value for money, etc.) and that both need to be assessed.

- The Public Complaints Bureau in Malaysia ensures that citizens are informed of their right to redress in annual reports, information clinics around the country, radio broadcasts and advertisements in local papers.

> **Client surveys in India and Uganda**
>
> In Bangalore, India, citizens and businesses complete 'report cards' in order to rate the public agencies which they use to solve problems or get services. The report cards, administered by the Public Affairs Centre in Bangalore, an NGO, assess the quality and cost of citizens' interactions with public agencies. In the first assessment of report cards, the Bangalore Development Authority, responsible for housing and other services, were rated as satisfactory by only one per cent of respondents. Rather than viewing this result as a threat, though, the authority's director took them as an opportunity, launching a citizen-government initiative to address delivery problems. Other agencies in Bangalore as well as groups in five other cities have also taken action inspired by the report card approach.
>
> The Ugandan Government is working with NGOs and communities carrying out surveys to obtain views on service delivery. The first survey found that just 11 per cent of rural households had ever been visited by an agricultural extension worker. Several districts have incorporated the survey findings into their district plans. One district has instituted further training for extension workers and is lobbying the central government for permission to spend more of its budget on extension workers.

Governments have found that by using the experience of citizens and involving them in monitoring and evaluating services, these approaches have helped to identify problems and implement innovative solutions resulting in better public sector performance.

- A 1997 survey undertaken for the Australian Public Service revealed that customers were quite clear about what was most important to them. In order of priority, these were:

    - the ability to speak to the right person;

    - fast and efficient service;

    - fair treatment;

    - friendly and courteous staff;

    - value for money;

    - access to and availability of facilities; and

    - the appearance and manner of staff.

As a result, public servants have been able to concentrate on making the changes that matter most to their clients, such as introducing 'main contact officers' who deal with all the different cases involving an allotted group of clients. These clients, in turn, are able to do all their business through one point of contact.

PUBLIC REPORTING

Public reporting is the practical means by which openness and transparency in government are improved. It is in keeping with a customer-orientated approach. Providing information on the financial and managerial performance of departments enables the public to understand and, where necessary, criticise or support what the public service is seeking to achieve. This encourages a sharing of national vision, values and aspirations and, in particular, stimulates an enhanced level of public expectations about public services.

- Malaysia's Public Complaints Bureau publishes an Annual Report which is available to the public together with a report on the administrative efforts undertaken by the Government and its progress.

Citizen orientation and encouraging feedback

Incorporated in Singapore's 'Public Service for the 21st Century' (PS21) initiative is an open pledge to the public that they will be given quality service. Feedback and suggestions are explicitly sought. The pledge is openly displayed in all government premises at all major points of contact with the public:

The Way of Excellence in Public Service
We want to give you quality service
We are courteous and fair
We do our best to help
We have pride in our work
We want to keep improving
Feedback shows us where we can do better
Suggestions help us improve
Praise helps us work with a smile
We need your trust, support and co-operation for
Excellence in Public Service

A PS21 Hotline has also been set up to garner feedback from the public about the quality of service delivery.

It is clear from a range of examples that, far from impeding the business of government, the effort expended on encouraging openness, citizen participation and improved customer service in the public sector reaps benefits that justify significant investments of time and money. Increased sensitivity to public demands and criticism facilitates the drive towards greater efficiency and, most significantly, identifies those areas most in need of reform. This is just as true for the core public sector as it is for privatised or state-owned enterprises.

Failure to invite public criticism will mean that service delivery can continue to run inefficiently and perform poorly without fear of reproach. Therefore, paradoxically, the most effective government departments are likely to be those which actively seek the most customer complaints. Governments need this pressure from its public in order to be sure that it is indeed the public interest that it is serving. Thus, although it may seem unhelpful initially, it will always ultimately be in the interests of government to set up mechanisms which facilitate public pressure on service delivery.

IMPROVING GOVERNMENT REGULATION

Regulation in its many forms – from parliamentary law to ministerial orders to municipal by-law – plays a vital role in serving and balancing the diverse interests and values of complex democratic societies and market economies. As an instrument of governance, regulations will continue to be used to meet a wide variety of legitimate social and economic needs. Yet there is growing evidence that reform of regulation, properly designed and carried out, can improve economic performance, and that potential effects of reform on other policy objectives, including public service delivery, can be better managed.

However, in many countries, the expansion of regulatory systems has given rise to concerns about:

- the growing quantity and costs of regulation;

- the quality of individual regulations; and

- the legitimacy and openness of regulatory decision processes.

QUANTITY AND COST

The number and complexity of regulations from all levels of government has continued to increase, threatening to overwhelm the capacity of both government administrations and private sectors. The cost of regulation is also rising, raising concern in many countries at a time of budget constraints. Further, the compliance costs borne directly by citizens and businesses are even greater. One solution used by some countries is the development of a new management framework to discipline and control regulation. Some countries have developed alternative and complementary policy instruments that can be more effective, less costly and more flexible.

- In New Zealand, deregulation is a key feature of the general programme of economic liberalisation which has eliminated most forms of restriction on entry to markets, removed price controls that formerly applied to a long list of items, and abolished regulatory monopolies and licensing that applied to many professions and trades. Deregulation can be seen as consistent with other reforms such as privatisation, simplified tax systems, and public sector finance reform.

THE NEED FOR BALANCE

Although the emphasis in recent decades has been on deregulation, concerns have grown over achieving the balance between minimal government intervention on the one hand whilst ensuring that sufficient regulation exists to protect the potential 'losers' in public sector downsizing. It is evident that not all areas of public service delivery can be left to the mercy of market forces. Prudent regulation of service delivery is essential if government is not to lose sight of its obligations to respect the rights of all citizens.

- The Government of Trinidad & Tobago has deemed regulation of public utilities to be necessary because of market failure. Regulation must, then, act as a substitute for competition, helping to achieve such results as would be evident in a free market setting. The Government recognises that regulation is essential to ensure the provision, by the public utilities, of adequate and safe services to all customers on equal terms at reasonable prices.

Regulation also assumes a renewed importance within the new paradigm of public service delivery. Managing a portfolio of different service providers, including those from the private sector, necessarily requires a certain amount of regulation from central government if both obligations to the public as a whole and government policy objectives are to be fulfilled.

- An example of the need to regulate services which have been contracted out comes from UK pension schemes. Many employees opt for an employer-based pension scheme over the state's supplementary pension provision, but although employer-based schemes must be approved by the tax authorities to ensure that such schemes are not just tax avoidance devices, there is very little government control over how these schemes operate. Thus, there have been a number examples of employer-based pension schemes which have been misused by the employer, or where the scheme had collapsed financially. The most famous of these was the Mirror Newspaper Group superannuation scheme whose funds were being diverted into the commercial activities of the Group.

So, whilst governments in recent years have rightly been concerned with reducing impediments to both efficient service provision and economic competitiveness, deregulation cannot be considered a panacea or guiding principle. The emphasis must be, above all, on quality regulation.

QUALITY

Quality regulation is crucial for government effectiveness and many countries have increased their attention to the quality of regulatory mechanisms. More broadly, they have also focused on the functioning of the administrative process through which regulations are developed, implemented, reviewed and revised.

Countries are also focusing on regulatory quality because the governing environment is changing. Economic conditions are becoming more difficult, and are highlighting direct and indirect costs of government actions. Businesses facing tougher competition are asking their governments to reduce regulatory burdens to the greatest extent possible. The quality of national regulatory systems is more important than ever to international competitiveness. New global markets and technologies have rendered some older forms of government regulation counter-productive. Internationalisation of regulation is also forcing governments to question long-standing regulatory traditions and to seek innovative forms of regulatory co-operation.

- Britain's Secretary of State for Employment declared, in 1986, that "we may not end with far fewer regulations but they will be better regulations." In Canada, the motto has been "regulating smarter".

Although experience from many countries suggests that good regulatory practices and techniques may significantly reduce burdens and improve effectiveness, it is not clear if the quality of regulations has improved over the past decade. Regulators' compliance with quality standards has been problematic in many cases, since it has proved difficult to establish incentives within bureaucracies for regulators to change their behaviour. Few countries have established any system for measuring regulatory improvement.

REGULATORY REFORM

The core objective of regulatory reform is better economic performance: increasing productivity, job creation and 'competitiveness', while retaining the public benefits of regulatory programmes. Countries seeking more dynamic and flexible economies are using reforms of both economic and social regulation to address a range of rigidities, disincentives, barriers to competition, and market distortions that reduce efficiencies at firm and sector levels. Efforts in some countries to reform regulations also address other economic objectives in particular to:

- Respond to *consumer needs, including those of user industries, and desires for lower prices, more choices, and increased convenience.* This is an important shift from regulatory regimes which have tended to protect producer groups at the expense of consumers and other users.

- Respond to *technological innovation* and more rapid product cycles in such sectors as communications, transport, and energy in order to support economic adaptation. Regulatory structures designed for outdated technologies penalise rather than protect consumers and user industries.

- Improve *government effectiveness*. If governments are to provide the framework to maximise economic wealth or to efficiently pursue important social objectives such as environmental quality and social cohesion, they must be capable of choosing the right policies, designing cost-effective regulatory instruments and approaches, and responding more quickly to change.

- *Improve the compatibility of national regulatory systems with a globalising economy.* As tariffs and quotas fall and the potential for trade expands, economic and social regulations assume greater importance as barriers to the flow of goods, services, investment or technology. International regulatory co-operation can produce economic gains from globalisation, such as fuller utilisation of economies of scale, while helping avoid unnecessary regulatory barriers to trade.

Deregulation and improved service to customers

The Registry of Companies and Businesses in Singapore has attempted to improve its service to clients in rectifying errors. Previously, the Companies Act provided for any particular recorded in a register which is erroneous to be rectified by a court order. To make it more convenient for members of the public to correct minor errors in their records, the Registry initiated a practice which allowed such errors to be dealt with by the straightforward lodging of a statutory declaration, thus bypassing the courts.

In 1990, the Malaysian Government undertook a survey of the system of licences and permits for business and investment. The survey revealed inefficiencies, delays and duplications. As a result initiatives were undertaken to issue composite licences, extend their period of validity, establish one-stop licensing centres, abolish certain licences and create exemptions to certain conditions for the granting of licences.

IMPLEMENTING BETTER REGULATIONS

A 1997 OECD report to government ministers made the following recommendations for achieving better quality regulation:

- Adopt regulatory reform policy at the highest political levels.

- Establish explicit standards for regulatory quality and principles of regulatory decision-making.

- Build capacities for central management and oversight of implementation of regulatory reform policy.

- Adopt processes for regulatory impact analysis.

- Open up the regulatory process to interested groups through a comprehensive policy on public consultation.

- Consider alternatives to regulation in a systematic way.

- Improve regulatory co-ordination so that multiple objectives are integrated.

- Review and evaluate the stock of existing regulations and paperwork.

- Reduce red tape and government formalities.

Improving the management of regulation must become an increasingly important focus for government action. Analysing the impact of regulatory systems as a whole, exploring cost-effective alternatives to regulation (e.g. economic incentives and information disclosure), and developing new arrangements which will guide the service towards its long-term goals, must become routine elements of the central management functions of government.

- In the UK, the Deregulation Initiative, dating back to 1985, but relaunched by the Prime Minister in 1992, has three key targets:

    - *better existing regulation*, to be achieved by cutting unnecessary burdens on business and streamlining existing requirements;

    - *better new regulation*, to be achieved by introducing new requirements only where necessary, minimising costs of compliance and consulting business about changes; and

    - *better enforcement of regulation*, to be achieved by ensuring that local authorities and national inspectorates apply regulations consistently, and provide guidance to make it easier for business to comply.

- In Canada, in 1992, the Treasury Board announced a new regulatory policy designed to address the problems of too many regulations which were making it difficult for Canada to compete in world markets, and the costs of implementation, given the decreasing public resources. The policy requires departments to consider a wide range of alternatives to regulation such as information campaigns, voluntary standards, persuasion, courses, self-regulation, ISO standards for management, market-based incentives and direct government expenditure before proceeding.

PROCEDURAL REFORMS

Deregulating administrative procedures relating to business enterprises needs to be supported and supplemented by improved internal systems and procedures. Awareness needs to be raised among departmental staff of the importance of removing bureaucratic red tape and its impact on their work processes, the organisation, their customers, and the economic development of the country.

Malaysia's Centre for Advisory Services

In Malaysia, deregulation in the public service has specifically focused on reducing red tape in administrative procedures relating to improving business activities. A one-stop centre called the 'Centre for Advisory Services,' part of the Malaysian Industrial Development Authority, provides investors with advice and the necessary approval for manufacturing licensees, tax incentives, and so forth, eliminating the obligation of going to various ministries and departments. Similar centres have also been set up at state level.

LESSONS LEARNED

Political, economic, social and institutional interests have hampered progress to improve regulatory processes and techniques. Moreover, regulatory management and reform have not been made any easier by regulatory inter-dependence. Governments no longer act in isolation; internationalisation and decentralisation have had major impacts on how they use their regulatory powers. However, successes in some countries as indicated above provide some grounds for optimism.

CONCLUSION

Public service reforms, of which a key component has been the rethinking of public service delivery, have been driven by economic pressures and by increasing expectations from consumers, and have been enabled by the renewed sense of managerial possibility which has emerged internationally. This possibility consists, as far as service delivery is concerned, of a wider range of alternative mechanisms and potential service providers than had previously been envisaged.

Maximising the potential within the new public service delivery paradigm depends on governments' capacity to afford, but also their willingness to manage new strategies. Where it is clear that improvements in both efficiency and service quality are to be had with the involvement of the private sector to varying degrees, it is the responsibility of government to mobilise this private sector. Privatisation, contracting out or partnership with NGOs need not be seen as a surrender of government responsibility in the interests of cost-cutting, but rather as part of a more strategic approach to public service delivery.

This publication has shown that the new approach must take into account a whole variety of factors and manifests itself in various ways. Quality management and the involvement of public servants in the renewal process are the origins of improved service delivery. The reorientation of the public service to a results-based focus then allows for a better assessment of which of the variety of potential mechanisms best suits the effective provision of a particular service. Innovations in the realm of information technology have also proved highly effective in contributing to improved service delivery. Structural change must also be reflected in a closer, more public focus on the particular needs of client citizens, and an emphasis on the values at the heart of a properly accountable civil service. Finally, a full reappraisal of regulatory controls on service providers needs to be undertaken in order to ensure that government neither restricts their autonomy too far nor allows them to neglect their duty to serve the larger public good.

In setting out the various practices for better service provision that have emerged across the Commonwealth in recent years, this publication has attempted to emphasise choice. As new techniques for best meeting citizens needs emerge, it is clear that developing countries have many more options to consider in building an effective public service than the industrialised nations have ever had in the past. Adopting techniques of customer service from abroad or from the private sector need not be indicative of a public service struggling to keep up with the demands placed on it. The Commonwealth experience shows that strategic management of public service delivery can ensure the place of the public sector at the forefront of the modernisation process.

BIBLIOGRAPHY

Current Good Practices and New Developments in Public Service Management: The Commonwealth Portfolio, Commonwealth Secretariat, 1996

Governance for the 21st Century: Lessons from Two Decades of Public Sector Reform, Commonwealth Secretariat, 1998

A Profile of the Public Service of Canada, Commonwealth Secretariat, 1994

A Profile of the Public Service of the United Kingdom, Commonwealth Secretariat, 1995

A Profile of the Public Service of Malaysia, Commonwealth Secretariat, 1995

A Profile of the Public Service of Malta, Commonwealth Secretariat, 1995

A Profile of the Public Service of Trinidad and Tobago, Commonwealth Secretariat, 1995

A Profile of the Public Service of New Zealand, Commonwealth Secretariat, 1995

A Profile of the Public Service of Zimbabwe, Commonwealth Secretariat, 1997

A Profile of the Public Service of the Republic of Singapore, Commonwealth Secretariat, 1998 (in preparation)

Alternative Service Delivery: Sharing Governance in Canada, edited by Robin Food and David Zussman (1997)

The Shifting Boundaries of Government: A United Kingdom International Conference, report by Sanford Borins, 1998